Rye Heritage Centre

Town Guide

Illustrated Guide to Rye
Ancient & Modern

Rye Heritage Centre

ILLUSTRATED RYE TOWN GUIDE

Contents

All About Rye Heritage Centre

The Rye Heritage Centre Charitable Incorporated Organisation (CIO)(Charity registration 1187978) was established in February 2020 to take on the operation of Rye Heritage Centre and to ensure the continued existence of the Rye Town Model, following the announcement of closure by the local council due to funding issues.

The Story of Rye is a 20 minute sound and lightshow which features the amazing room sized 1:100 scale model of the town as it was in Victorian times, built by Joy and Ted Harland over nearly four years in the early 1970s. The sound and light show was fully updated in 2023 by the charity with energy efficient lighting and additional projection imagery. The model was thoroughly cleaned, repaired and re-assembled giving new life to an important heritage asset.

The centre also houses a private collection of old Penny Arcade machines such as might have been found on and early 20thcentury seaside pier, these machines have been maintained and repaired and can still be played on today.

Newly added in 2024 is the Smuggler's Attic – come and see a fun multi-media experience introducing the visitor to the area's rich history of smuggling.

Of course, no heritage centre would be without interesting and informative displays interpreting the area's heritage, both for the visitor and the local community.

As a small independent charity we depend on visitors and donations to survive.

If you'd like to find out more about us or donate to our funding please scan the QR code below or visit www.ryeheritage.co.uk

You can email us at info@ryeheritage.co.uk
or call us on 01797 331066

Come and see the amazing Rye Town Model

Maps

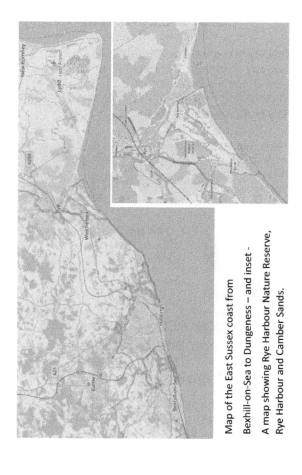

Map of the East Sussex coast from
Bexhill-on-Sea to Dungeness – and inset -

A map showing Rye Harbour Nature Reserve,
Rye Harbour and Camber Sands.

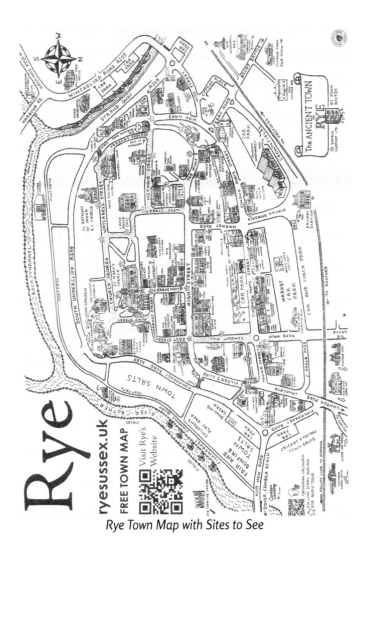

Rye Town Map with Sites to See

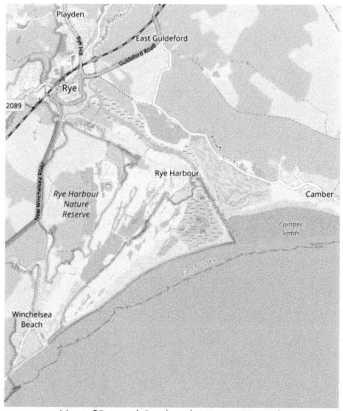

Map of Rye and Camber showing main roads

Preface

Dear Reader

Rye Heritage Centre welcomes you to Rye.

We hope you have a great holiday or day out. Our guide will help you to understand the past and present of our wonderful Cinque Port town. Rye has been through many crises and at times it looked as though the town could not survive. But the great resilience of the people of Rye shone through as you will read below. Hard work and inspiration saved Rye and so its vibrant legacy is here for you today.

Rye is a special place for you to enjoy, visited by over one million people each year. This is a town that has everything: sea, sky, wildlife and plant life, rivers and shorelines, impressive buildings, fascinating cobbled streets, churches, shops, cafes and restaurants, museums and art galleries; a history of literary associations, terrifying storms, tales of heroism, witchcraft, ghost stories and notorious characters including pirates and smugglers; footpaths and coastal tracks, cycleways, roads and parking places, a bus service, railway station and harbour. Most importantly Rye has an amazing history for a small town, as we hope you will soon discover. Please take the time to look around our Heritage Centre and see the **Story of Rye** - a sound and light show featuring the incredible **Rye Town Model**, our heritage displays and, of course, spend a few minutes in **The Smuggler's Attic**! We welcome questions and suggestions.

Kind regards **Rye Heritage Centre**

The Most Important Sites in Rye

Below is an alphabetical list of the sites to look for during your visit or stay. Most are marked on the map above. This Guide's narrative history of Rye details their formation and context.

In the chart below, these sites are arranged by the century of their probable origin based on research in historic records.

A section of short historic details about each building or location follows the chart.

In this Guide we have used the Old English lettering for the Saxon era – so 'Æthelred the Unready' rather than 'Ethelred' and we have standardised the spelling of 'Baddyngs'

Augustine Friar's Monastery

Baddyngs Gate

Camber Castle

Church Square

Cinque Ports Street

Conduit Hill

Custom House - West Street (formerly Grene Hall)

Ferry Road & Tollgate

First Cinema - The Electric Palace

First Regent Cinema and Second

Fishmarket

Fletcher's House

Flushing Inn

Friars of the Sack

George Hotel

Girl's School (now KINO Cinema)

Gun Garden

High Street

Huckstep's Row

Jeake's House

Lamb House

Needle's Passage

Old Police Station

Postern Gate

Pump Street – Church Square

Rye Grammar School

Rye Heritage Centre

Rye Railway Station

Rye River Barges

EARLIEST TIMES

Neolithic flints
Ancient pottery
Early coins
Skeletal remains
Strand Quay (Roman era?)
Harbour area - The Camber
Fishmarket (c.700 CE)

CENTURIES

10th
Origin of Rameslie – before 982
Rye River Barges (probably from Norman designs)

11th
Donation of Rameslie (1023-33) to 1247
St Mary's Church in Market Street (foundation probably pre-1085)

12th
Rye's original Minting coin centre
The Mermaid Inn

13th
Ypres Tower
Friars of the Sack (1263)
Royal Charter (1278)

14th
First Austin Priory 1364 (destroyed c.1377).
2nd Augustine Friar's Monastery (1379)
Conduit Hill
Landgate
Strand Gate
Postern Gate
Baddyngs Gate
Old Bell Inn
Turkey Cock Lane
Church clock components (c.1368)

15th
St Anthony's (Wealden Hall House)
Watchbell Street
Church Square (some buildings)
Cinque Ports Street

16th
Camber Castle
Church Clock (installation 1562)
George Hotel
Gun Garden

16TH – continued

Fletcher's House
Flushing Inn
High Street
Huckstep's Row
Needle's Passage
Pump Street – Church Square
The Water Pump and Reservoir
Windmills

17th
Jeake's House
Rye Grammar School (1636)
Ship Inn

18th
Lamb House (1722)
Custom House
Ferry Road & Tollgate
The Mint
Tiilingham Windmill (Gibbets Marsh)
The Town Hall

19th
Rye Railway Station
Rye Gasworks
Girl's school (now KINO cinema)

20th
Old Police Station
First cinema - the Electric Palace
First Regent Cinema *and second*
St Anthony Padua Church
War Memorial
Rye Heritage Centre

Historic Sites of Rye by Century

The Gun Garden

Mermaid Street

Description of Historic Sites

Description of Historic Buildings

Augustine Friar's Monastery

The Austin Friars had been welcomed to England from Tuscany by Jew-hating King Henry III around 1248. By about 1330, Austins, the last large group of hermit monks to come from Italy to England had twenty-two houses in England and five in Ireland. By the time of the terrible Black Death (1348-49) there were around five hundred Austin Friars in England. Women also lived as nuns under the Rule of St Augustine and by 1387 the number of Augustine English convents was between thirty-eight and forty-four.

Our local community of hermits arrived in Rye from Italy around 1364, welcomed by King Edward III and Rye townsfolk. The original monastery was abandoned due the predations of the sea as well as fear of French attacks. During the Hundred Years War with France (1337-1453), raiders came across the English Channel to ravage Rye. After a particularly vicious attack in 1377, a new Austin Friary with a garden was built at 'le Haltone' in Conduit Street, now called Conduit Hill, inside the protective walls of Rye town; it was probably completed in 1380, in the reign of King Richard II. During this turbulent time, two hundred oak trees were cut from Fore Wood in Crowhurst for the monks to shore up Rye's defences.

The friars, who wore black robes, were known formally as the Hermits of the Order of St Augustine formed in Tuscany, Italy in 1244 on the instructions of Pope Innocent IV, but now more commonly as 'Austin Friars'. Following King Henry VIII's Acts of Supremacy in 1534, the monastery community was then dissolved in 1538 and the monastery fell into disrepair, but the Chapel remained as a useful building.

Once the enforced Dissolution took place, the Chapel building became an especially useful community resource. It has served as a brewer's malt house, and a store for vital salt and other provisions. The great English wool trade was partly successful because of vast numbers of sheep on Romney Marsh and so the chapel has also been a wool store. Following the formation of the Salvation Army in 1865, the chapel became their barracks until the Citadel in Rope Walk became their new home (now an antique shop). The Church of England then used the chapel as a Sunday School. Reverend Howes, Vicar of Rye suggested it became a 'Church House'; after alterations it was opened in 1905. In World War II, the Rye community took it over for dances. When Rye's cinema was bombed by the Nazis, the Chapel continued the film shows. It showed its flexibility once again on 30th May 1964 when it was taken over by Cinque Ports Pottery until July 2007 as Rye became a leading ceramics centre. It has undergone much renovation and restoration work between 2015 and 2023 and is now a private residence doubling up as a high-end antiques and interiors showroom.

Baddyngs Gate

This is named after the single Rye Ward now called Baddings in modern parlance. Over time the spelling of the name has varied – being Baddyng's Gate with apostrophe and Baddyngs Tower without the apostrophe. The ward elects 16 members, one of whom is chosen as the Mayor of Rye. However, because the Ypres Tower is in Baddyngs Ward, it was also called Baddyngs Tower. The standard spelling in this Guide is Baddyngs.

Camber Castle

This Grade I castle was built in the 16th century. It was also known as Winchelsea Castle – a Device Fort against French attacks. When it was first built in the period 1512 to 1514 the sea area called the Camber Anchorage was right next to it. King Henry VIII decided that as the threat from France grew, so the fort was too small, and it was expanded to a four-bastioned stone castle by the Moravian engineer Stefan von Haschenperg.

The king authorised twenty-eight artillery guns to be operated by a small garrison commanded by a captain. The sea soon silted up the harbour area and the castle became of less use as the guns could not reach the enemy at sea. However, it was manned until 1637 and then closed on the orders of King Charles I. When Oliver Cromwell realised that he risked a Royalist castle near vital Rye Harbour, he partly demolished the castle. The romantic ruin was painted by JMW Turner and became a favourite picnic spot with much wildlife. Turner also used the castle as a vantage point for several other paintings including the well-known view of Rye itself. It was privately-owned until 1977 when English Heritage took it over and began repairs. The Castle is currently deemed to be in too dangerous a condition to allow public access to the interior, the exterior can be seen from the adjacent footpath.

Church Square

The most important buildings in this square are number 54 to 60, all listed as worthy of conservation by Historic England.

Cinque Ports Street

The five Cinque Ports, Sandwich, Dover, Hythe, Romney, and Hastings were formally grouped in the time of King Edward the Confessor, but Rye was not included originally. However, as you may read later in this guide, Rye's time as a Cinque Port naval defender of England first began when Rye and Winchelsea, called the Two Antient Towns, became 'limbs' of the head port of Hastings between1150-1199. The original five ports had many privileges including running their own courts and punishments and managing the great Herring Fairs at Yarmouth. It was King Henry II in 1189 who gave Rye and Winchelsea the same privileges as the five but not the same status. All the seven ports had to supply men and ships for 'ship service' to the king for a fixed number of days a year plus any emergencies. By 1229, Rye was supplying five ships to the king on a regular basis. When Hastings declined in the 1300s, Rye and Winchelsea became Cinque Ports with full status and privileges. The Cinque Ports Coat of Arms was granted by the king in 1305. Probably their greatest achievements have been the victory over the French fleet led by Eustace the Monk in 1216 and the huge army transport of ten thousand men to Harfleur leading to victory in the Battle of Agincourt, according to John Collard in his book *A Maritime History of Rye*.

Conduit Hill

Our Friary hermits could not rely entirely on charity to survive in Rye. The first task was to ensure a sound water supply. The monks found fresh water just outside the town wall. A pump was installed in the pumphouse at the top of Rope Walk and a 'conduit' was made of wooden pipes, carrying the water to the Church Yard reservoir. At the foot of Conduit Hill stood the Postern Gate – the pedestrian access to the town.

Custom House - West Street (formerly Grene Hall)

The Custom House dates to around 1790-1810 but the north face of the building was converted to a mock timber frame by Ernest Trobridge. The carriageway arch is still preserved and it has a casement window. It is a Grade II Listed building and is a good example of the use of mathematical tiles which give the impression the building is of brick construction rather than timber framed.

Ferry Road & Tollgate

The Toll Gate on this road was used to charge fees for various
types of transport such as wagons and coaches. The road
itself has many interesting properties which have preservation
orders upon them. These are Nos 2 to 6, and 9 to 11 Ferry
Road. The former Rye Primary School was sited here near
the railway crossing, demolished in 1998 and at the time of
writing still awaiting redevelopment after decades of laying
waste. The Ferry Boat Inn dated to 1700 and remarkably had
a one-thousand-year lease. It was leased by Edward Doge who
was from Ebony in Kent. He built a house and some stables here
in his trade as a carpenter.

First cinema - the Electric Palace

Rye's first cinema was opened in 1910 and there are
photographs showing eyewatering failures of health and safety
as the building was formed without scaffolding or safety nets for
workers. It was known as 'The Flea Pit' to Ryers. In 1923, since
cinemas were extremely popular, the Shipman & King Circuit of
cinemas took it over, only to close it in 1932 in order to feature
their new building, the Regent Cinema. The Electric Palace now
acts as a commercial property.

First Regent Cinema and second

The first Regent Cinema, designed by Henry Couzens of
Hastings, opened in 1932 and had 671 seats. In 1942, just as
the assistant manager was finishing a training show, Hitler's
Luftwaffe bombed the cinema, and he was killed. The ruins were
left for another six years and then in 1948 the second cinema
was born out of the ashes - the designer this time being David
Nye. He managed to build in 744 seats with a banked tier system
and no balcony. The cinema opened on 11th March 1948, then
was taken over by EMI in 1967, and was closed in 1973. The empty
building was demolished, and in 1984 it was replaced by the
Regent Motel.

Fishmarket

Rye fish market is located now on Simmons Quay, but it has been located in many places to suit the sea, tides and harbour docking requirements. Rye has always been a town for fishing and historians have commented on the link between the old word Rie and the Ripiers who would supply fish to the monarch in London. A cine film was made back in 1960 showing how the fisherfolk and their market worked. It is most certainly still working with fresh fish being landed each day. You can stand on the harbour arm at Rye Harbour and watch the fishing boats going in and out on the tides.

Heritage photograph of Rye Harbour with fishing vessels and paddle steamer

Fletcher's House

Fletcher's House, currently a restaurant, is reputed to be the birthplace of John Fletcher, an Elizabethan dramatist and playwright who is known to have collaborated with Shakespeare. John's father was Minister at the nearby church and was a real "fire and brimstone" preacher who went on to be Dean of Peterborough and then Bishop of London. The facade of the building is relatively modern but the building itself is of Tudor origin and contains some significant timber work and original Tudor doorways with carved Tudor roses in the frame.

Flushing Inn

The Flushing Inn is located on Market Street in Rye. The first Flushing Inn was destroyed by the French in 1377. This now has the address No 4 and it is the location of a true tragedy. It was here the butcher John Breads had his home. In 1742, Breads murdered Alan Grebell by mistake instead of his intended victim, the town's mayor. He was the last man to be hanged in Rye, in 1743, and his body was exhibited in a gibbet cage which is normally kept in the attic of the Town Hall complete with the remains of his skull. A replica hangs in the auditorium of the Story of Rye at Rye Heritage Centre. The building is remarkable also for its cellar dating back to Norman times and the building over the cellar dates to the late 1300s having been rebuilt after the 1377 French raid. Another feature is the Tudor fresco found behind a wall in 1905, It was restored when found and again in 1961 by English Heritage due to fading. The Flushing Inn is now a private residence.

Friars of the Sack

In 1801 John Vidler bought this building and it has a long connection to Vidler family ownership. It is not known why or how the building is connected to the Friars of the Sack, but their background is that they were called the Friars of the Penance of Jesus Christ, formed in 1245. They came to London in 1257 at the invitation of King Henry III. The Pope suppressed the Italian section of the Order in 1274 after it amalgamated with other penitent orders, however we know that the English section existed after that in London and did come to Rye c.1263. The English section of the order was dissolved around 1307.

George Hotel

The George Hotel as an entity was moved here from another building in 1719 and is made of components of different dates. Some of it dates to an earlier building of the 16th century, some to the 18th century and the ballroom was added in 1818. This was previously the farmer's assembly room on market days. It has an amazing history, with three kings called George allegedly staying here according to the hotel management, along with the Mayor of London. It is where the post coach picked up and dropped the mail to and from London from around 1778. It was the town's principal meeting house and later its masonic lodge in the Benson Room. It was renovated between 2004 and 2006 but badly damaged by fire in 2019. Extensive rebuilding took place over the next few years and it was re-opened in May 2022.

Girl's school (now KINO cinema)

Originally a Victorian school, the cinema was built on the site of the former library and adult education centre at the top of Lion Street. Initially, the historical site was earmarked for housing, but local opposition led to its preservation. A community group stepped in and pledged hundreds of thousands of pounds to save part of the building from demolition. It was turned into a two-screen 150-seater cinema which opened in 2015 and has sold 280,000 tickets and shown 1,000 different films. It has been known as 'The Heart of Rye' because of its popularity.

Gun Garden

The Gun Garden lays in front of the mid-13th century town castle called the Ypres Tower where one of the two parts of the Rye Museum are located. It was not part of the original castle design but was ordered to be constructed by King Henry VIII as part of the Rye defences along with Camber Castle. When he died and Elizabeth I came to fear the Spanish Armada, it was refurbished and rearmed in 1588 and then later more weapons were added to fight the French in the 18th century. It kept its weapons right up to 1830 when it had eighteen guns. Now the cannons and cannonballs are for show.

High Street

Why not stand in the High Street and picture a bustling thoroughfare from past centuries full of piratical smugglers, drunken oafs, and women of the night, or perhaps orderly religious and civic processions with people in wonderful uniforms and dresses. Today there is little left in the way of traditional high street shops as the town has evolved into a tourism-based economy. Key buildings being conserved are 1 and 1A, 79 and 80, 99 and 100, 111 and 112.

Huckstep's Row

This alleyway between houses originally led to properties that were once described as 'unsightly excrescences'. The Borough Corporation had set out a policy at the beginning of the 20th century to carry out remedial work to remove numerous eyesores by embarking on a programme of slum clearance, demolition and refurbishment. This was to signal, in the 1930s, the beginnings of the indigenous population of Rye resettling outside the Town Walls. To come were the housing estates of King's Avenue and Tilling Green. Huckstep's Row was colloquially known as Fishgut Alley where some 20 large families, engaged in maritime and shoreline activities, sought out a basic existence in poverty and squalor - hard to believe when you now view the opulence and grandeur of nearby properties valued in excess of a million pounds!

During the 1930s the builders moved in and began the transformation into what we see today, some would say this completed the gentrification of the area referred to as the Citadel (within the Town Walls) following similar post Great War improvements in the town. The area then became a centre for literature when the writer Radclyffe Hall and her partner, sculptor Lady Troubridge lived in the Row including the house called the Forecastle. It is sad to note that

these well-meaning rehousing programmes led eventually
to division and resentment within the community between
the descendants of families who had gladly accepted better
conditions and the wealthy occupants and second home
owners of the modern day 'citadel'.

Jeake's House

The remarkable Jeake's House in Rye originally belonged to the
Jeake family, of Huguenot origin. At one time it was a wool
store and warehouse just like our Austin Friar's Chapel. The
home's foundation was laid at exactly midday on 13th June 1689
when the heavenly bodies charted were in the right position.
The reason for this is that Samuel Jeake, the builder, was an
all-round genius and polymath who was an astrologer, as well as
a Christian Puritan. Visitors and stayers have been many, but we
can select Elizabeth Fry, the prison reformer, author E F Benson
and poet T S Eliot for example.

Lamb House

Much of Rye's heritage has depended on the wine trade with
extensive cellars and shipping to and from Gascony and often,
the stealing of wine cargoes of other nations. Lamb House is
an example of the benefits of the wine trade as it was built
in 1722 by James Lamb who made his fortune from wine and
politics. Four years after the house was built, King George I was
shipwrecked at Camber Sands and came to stay with Lamb.
Then, in 1897 the novelist Henry James came to live here until
1916, when the brothers A C and E F Benson, who wrote the
Mapp and Lucia novels, moved in. In 1950 the house was given
to the National Trust as a writers' museum and remains in their
safe custodianship.

Lamb House

Needle's Passage

This is a link from Cinque Ports Street to The Mint and was almost certainly used by the violent smugglers that populated Rye and who terrified the public into silence while the Revenue Men gave endless chase, often ending in their murder. Once known as Venell's passage after the owners of an adjacent property the passageway is technically private and traditionally is closed one day a year to prevent its adoption as a public right of way. One step has the date 1936 imprinted and local legend says it is unlucky to tread on the step - many locals still adhere to this superstition.

Old Police Station

The instigator of law and order in recent times was William H Balls, an Irishman who came to Rye around 1850. He helped to set up a police department and he worked with the police for 30 years. By the 1920s there was a constant police presence and eventually they had a large area to patrol with nine constables to cover from Northiam south to Broomhill and Rye.

Postern Gate

This was the main pedestrian entrance to the town of Rye.

Pump Street – Church Square

Around five hundred years ago, a water supply system was set up with a cistern at the top of the hill and using a wooden-boxed lead pump. You can see what is left of the apparatus now with its Rye Corporation date of a new pump – 1826. The pipe behind the grill is called a 'Rat's Tail.'

Rye Grammar School

The old Rye Grammar School building was erected in 1636 by Thomas Peacocke (sometimes written 'Pecock'), perhaps a few years before his death. Peacock's Will described this building as 'a house' but the layout suits the requirements of a school. He willed it to the town in the period between 1638 and 1644 and in the latter year it was legally conveyed to Rye Town ownership. However, our national archives reveal that a previous Grammar School had already been formed in Rye since the (still existing) early school records begin in 1634 and continued until 1845. To complicate matters further, the original school had two headmasters and was known as 'Peacocke's and Sanders'. It was a free grammar school for boys until 1908 when a new Thomas Peacocke School was built elsewhere. Rye Grammar School and Rye Secondary School were converted to a single comprehensive school in the period between 1967 and 1969. Later it became a Community College. The old Rye Grammar School building was taken over as a record shop in 1991.

Old Grammar School Commemorative Plaque

Rye Heritage Centre

The Centre focuses on all aspects of the past in our amazing town of Rye. We host the 'Story of Rye' Town Model with its Sound and Light show and the Smuggler's Attic, together with a variety of displays and exhibits interpreting the long and rich heritage of the area. The huge town model was built over three years by two local residents between 1973 and 1976 and is undoubtedly one of the country's most detailed and accurate scale models. Outside on the cobbles is a giant ship's anchor, dredged up from the seabed and thought to be from a 13th to

15th century warship of similar size to the Mary Rose. The Centre is situated on the historic Strand Quay where in medieval days the merchant ships would dock. Eventually the tide semaphore system was installed and operated to show boats when it was safe to come upriver.

Rye Railway Station

During a period of railway expansion across the whole of England, engineers drew up plans to bring the railway from Ashford to Rye back in the early 1840s. It took ten years of challenging work for contractor New Haven Railroad to lay the track. The first train arrived on 28th October 1850, before the station building designed by William Tress was opened, on 13th February 1851. It survived the Beeching cuts of 1963 and operates a vital service today. Mitchell and Smith in their South Coast Railway's state '...when Parliament was considering plans for railways to Hastings, it opted for a line from Ashford as it would be strategically advantageous as a means of protecting the 'open door' [in defence terms]. The South Eastern Railway thus had to accept that it was not likely to be a profitable route.'

Rye River Barges

It is thought that the design of the Rye barges that plied the Rother, Tillingham and Brede rivers could well be based on the transport barges of the Norman invasion fleet of 1066, giving them a history of almost one thousand years! Of course our barges were made in Rye shipyards, and serviced many communities from Rye Harbour to Bodiam, Winchelsea, Brede and the King's shipyard village of Smallhythe. The carrying of coal to fuel the giant steam pumping engines at Brede continued until the advent of road haulage in the early 20th century. Rye barges also used the Royal Military Canal built to help defeat Napoleon. They carried everything from sand and ballast to manure and bricks, as well as wood from the Wealden Forest, hops and hop poles, and even wool, glass, and livestock. There is one remaining barge in Hastings Shipwreck Heritage Centre that was rescued from a mudflat where it had lain since the 1930s. This is being refurbished. Her name is Primrose, and she was built in 1890 near Strand Quay.

Ship Inn

Because of the government's decision to tax imports and exports of valuable commodities such as wool and tea, smuggling became rife with many battles between the coastal patrols such as the Revenue Men and the hard-faced and often vicious smugglers of the area. When contraband was seized it had to be stored somewhere. The building known now as the Ship Inn was built as a contraband warehouse in 1592. Seized goods were sold off here at period auctions and alcohol was sold for refreshment at later auctions, eventually the warehouse became an established inn, The Ship Inn, which still has the 16th century beams preserved in its rooms.

St Anthony of Padua Church

This is a Roman Catholic church built unusually in the Spanish-Romanesque style between 1927 and 1929, for the Conventual Franciscans on the site of an older church called St Walburga's dated to 1900. St Walburga's was demolished in 1927 and the large new church was designed by John Mendham and opened on 30th June 1929.

St Anthony's (Wealden Hall House)

St Anthony's Wealden Hall is a certain style of building built in medieval times by well-off yeomen farmers as a timber-framed hall usually with a central building and two wings with walls covered in wattle and daub. This is one of many Wealden Halls built in the two hundred years from 1300 to 1500. The insulation is interesting to say the least as it is made of an imaginative mixture of earth, dung, and horsehair with a flooring of chalk mixed with sour milk that turned into a kind of concrete. This particular Wealden Hall in Rye was built as a farmer's house after the Black Death.

St Mary's Church in Market Street

This is a beautiful and fascinating church, and a climb up
through the bell loft to the top of the tower spire will give you
access to amazing views across the land and seascape. Located
in the Manor of Rameslie given to the Norman Abbey of Fecamp
before the Conquest of 1066, the church is of Norman origin
and is the oldest building in Rye, completed circa 1135. There
is some evidence in French national archives that the Abbot
of Fecamp, called Little John, came to Rye to advise on the
founding of the new stone church in 1085 on his way to Steyning
to meet King William the Conqueror and his sons. There was
probably a wooden Saxon church on this site at the top of Rye's
pyramidal hill dating back to c.600 CE. The church, like the rest
of Rye was raided and burned in 1377 and the roof collapsed
once the lead was stolen. The bells were taken to two villages
on the French coast and recovered the next year together with
much plunder. Both French villages were burned in retribution.

St Mary's Church Garden

There is a mystery to the manufacture and fitting of St Mary's old clock. Church records confirm that it was installed by the French Huguenot refugee, Lews Billiard in the years 1561-2, that much is certain. Billiard worked as an apprentice for Alan Bawdyson, the Royal Clockmaker to Elizabeth I. He was paid £30.00 for his work. This is worth £11,768.00 today. However, following recent investigations, the clock may not have been made originally for Rye's famous church. It has been shown by an expert from Cumbria Clocks that the mechanism in the glass case (shown in the photograph) is so similar to the ancient clocks in Salisbury and Wells Cathedral which were made in the 14th century that our Rye clock is likely to be much older that 1562. It could be the oldest clock in the world, vying with that of Padua in Italy (c.1348). There was even a friendly but competitive claim by the folk of Winchelsea that the clock now at St Mary's was really the one they purchase for their own great church of St Thomas of Canterbury in 1388. There is also evidence that Hampton Court Palace had a Royal clock like this and it could have been sold to Rye. Research into the clock's history is still going on. Whatever the truth of the matter, there is a document showing that Lewys Billiard was paid for his installation work at Rye. Some horologist experts deny that there is sufficient similarity between the Salisbury Clock and the Rye clock and so the saga goes on. If you select the link to the Clock Controversy in the Weblinks page you will be able to read the full facts about this marvellous timepiece.

The remarkable clock of St Mary's Church

St Mary's Church comments:

'It is one of the oldest church turret clocks in the country still functioning. The pendulum, a much later addition, swings in the body of the church. The present exterior clockface and the original 'Quarter Boys' (so called because they strike the quarters but not the hours) were added in 1760/1. Today, if you wish, you can climb the church tower where you will see the 8 bells now hanging there. These are not the same bells that were stolen in 1377 as they were re-cast in 1775 and new bells added. The total weight of the 8 bells and clappers is almost 5 tons.'

The church is listed as Grade I by English Heritage.

St Mary's Church bell loft

Strand Gate

The Strand Gate has now been destroyed but like the Landgate it was part of Rye's defences at the seaward edge of the town – The Strand is where the ships docked in medieval times. Slowly the longshore drift accumulated shingle, sand and silt, keeping the sea edge far out into the bay, so that Rye was no longer almost an island. The location of the Strand Gate was next to the Mint which it is believed was still operational in 1115. This is evidenced by the recent find of a large hoard of Rye's coins about forty miles north of Paris.

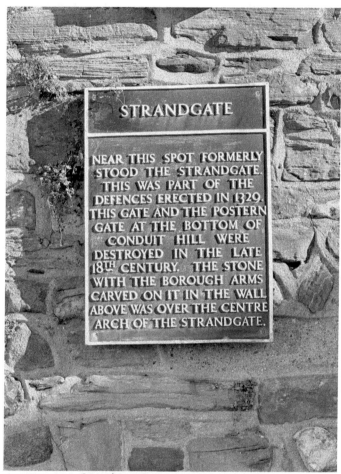

Strandgate Commemorative Plaque

The Landgate

The iconic Landgate has stood here since the reign of King
Edward III (reigned 1327-1377), and is nearly seven hundred years
old; having lost its roof a long time ago it is now in constant

danger of being defeated by pigeon poo! In 2015, five tonnes of pigeon guano were removed from the arch, the exercise being repeated several times since. Back in the day of King Edward III, the fortified arch had a portcullis, large gates, and a drawbridge. A clock was added in Victorian times to commemorate Prince Albert, the mechanism now inoperable, having also succumbed to nesting pigeons. At the time of writing the clock is known to show the correct time just twice a day.

The Landgate

The Landgate from the north

The Mermaid Inn

The cellars of this remarkable inn were built in 1156 and the main structure in 1420 on the site of the earlier inn. This inn was a favourite meeting place for the Hawkhurst Gang of smugglers, who drank to excess with their feet up on the tables. This famous Inn was visited by the author Russel Thorndyke; here he found inspiration for stories in his series of Dr Syn novels written about a fictional smuggler who operated in the Rye and Romney Marsh area. Inside you'll also see evidence of Shakespeare's visits and more. This inn has so many ghost stories told about it that it is worth reading the tales on their website – a very scary place. One visitor locked his room and went out into the street and looking up he saw a man and woman in his room staring back at him from his window.

Mermaid Inn

The Mint

This street probably never actually hosted a Mint making coins. It was given this name by over-romantic Victorians. However, there was a real Mint somewhere in Rye which operated during the reign of King Stephen (1136-1145) which must have been frightening as it was the time of The Anarchy with fighting and horrific torture described in the Anglo-Saxon Chronicle. The name of the coin maker or 'moneyer' was Raulf and a silver penny has been found that was made by this moneyer which is on display in Rye Museum. This is a very rare coin with only ten examples known anywhere.

The Olde Bell Inn

This very old public house in Mint Street is named after the 1378 raid on France when the town bells stolen by the French were recovered by men of Rye and Winchelsea. The original building was constructed in 1390 and still has the original oak beams in the ceiling and wooden floors. This inn has a fascinating history of smuggling as it contains a revolving cupboard used by smugglers for a fast getaway. The cupboard is rumoured to connect an underground tunnel to the Mermaid Inn. So, the notorious Hawkhurst Gang (1730-1740) may well have been able to flee from inn to inn if the Revenue men were in hot pursuit.

The Town Hall

This is the town's third Town Hall. There was a medieval wooden building used as the original Town Hall, but it was burned down with the rest of the town during the Hundred Years War with France in June 1377. Then a replacement was made in the period 1378 to 1741. This was then dismantled and a new Town Hall designed by Andrews Jelfe was built on this spot in 1742 and has been here ever since. The Town Hall contains some fascinating artefacts including a scale mode of the current building and a pillory last used in 1813 to punish a man who helped the French prisoner General Philipon to escape. Most notoriously there is the Rye Gibbet Cage used to hang the murderer John Breads in chains on the Gibbet Marsh. Breads' bones were seen as a cure for rheumatism so some were stolen. The current building also served as Rye Magistrates Court until the 1990s.

Rye Town Hall

The Town Wall

As mentioned above, the town had a defensive wall which stretched from Baddyngs Gate to Strand Gate. Not much remains of it today, however the best remaining section can be seen at the back of the car park on Cinque Ports Street.

The Water Reservoir (Cistern)

The proper name of this remarkable feature is the Rye Water House. It was at least one hundred years ahead of its time, dating to the 16th century, and it gave Rye a cistern and water tank to avoid local residents having to collect water by hand from a well. The Dome covered the underground reservoir and had pipes made of Elm trees in 1733 so that the water was no longer contaminated by lead. Then in the late 1700s more pipes were added to take water from the old Postern Gate to St Mary's churchyard via Conduit Hill. Water pressure was maintained with a new pump in 1826, positioned as it is today, on the corner of Tower Street and Rope Walk. But Rye eventually needed more water, so a borehole was drilled at Cadborough Cliff in 1898 and then in 1935 a concrete reservoir was placed on Rye Hill to increase the water pressure once more. The old well with the name of Budge was closed in 1969.

The Water Reservoir known as The Cistern

Turkey Cock Lane

Death by Starvation – for the Sake of Love. A famous ghost story of Rye concerns an Austin Friar, appropriately named

'Cantata', who fell in love with Amanda, a local girl. She became enamoured of his beautiful singing, and they eloped but were recaptured. Strictly against the rules of the religious order Cantata was punished by being bricked into a wall cavity in what is now called Turkey Cock Lane, to starve to death. In some ghostly versions, the skeletons were still locked in each other's arms, with noises of their dying breath being heard at night, supposedly sounding like turkeys. However, allegedly one male body was found in the cavity during World War II. Amanda may have passed away broken-hearted shortly after her lover died in the cavity.

War Memorial

Strangely the War Memorial in St Mary's churchyard does not commemorate the bravery and huge loss of life of Rye's ship crews in their many Cinque Ports battles with the French and Spanish. However, it most certainly does pay homage to those who lost their lives in the First and Second World wars and the Gulf and Iraq wars. The memorial was designed by Sir Reginald Blomfield and was unveiled in 1919. It is made of Bath stone and a bronze sword is mounted on its front face. The memorial details the names of the 142 citizens lost between 1914 and 1918 as well as the names of those who sacrificed their lives for us in subsequent wars. Sir Reginald designed several other significant buildings in his home town of Rye but is best known for his design for the Menin Gate in Ypres.

Watchbell Street

During the Hundred Years War with France in 1377, a fleet raid against Rye was led by Castilian admiral Ferdinando Sanches de Tovar and French Admiral of All France, Jean de Vienne. During this raid, the town was burned, the women raped, the lead from the church roof of St Mary's stolen, along with its bells. In the following year, the ships of Rye and Winchelsea attacked the French coast and recovered the bells to return to the church. One was retained and mounted in a frame at the end of the street. The bell you see today comes from a nearby village church and has been placed near the western lookout to remind us that in days of old, the bell was rung as a warning if the French were spotted returning to plunder the town.

The Watchbell

Windmills

Rye Windmill on Gibbet's Marsh stands just by the River Tillingham tide gates. There has been a windmill on this site for at least five hundred years. Records are not complete, but the first recorded owner was Thomas Chatterton with his post mill of 1758. This was demolished after his death in 1820, to make a smock mill like the one there now. The mill worked until 1920 and then was taken over by a bakery but on an unlucky Friday 13th in 1930 the overheated ovens set fire to the windmill. The wood burned but the brick base did not, so like the phoenix the mill rose again from its ashes in 1932 and baking recommenced until 1976.

Windmill on the River Tillingham

Ypres Tower

This is Rye's small town castle, initially planned by a knight
known as 'The Little Charlemagne' - Count Peter II of Savoy
(1203-1268) between 1226 and 1249, to be much larger castle .
It now takes its name from the later purchaser from Kent, John
de Ypres in 1430. During the 16th century it was often used to
keep prisoners and a full-time gaoler was appointed in 1796.
The authorities gave the prisoners an exercise yard, and then
it was expanded to include a women's prison in 1837. It ceased
being a prison in 1891, becoming a morgue instead. This Grade
1 building is now one of the two sites of Rye Museum. It was
also called Baddyngs Tower. Below the tower was the sites of
the original Baddyngs Gate.

Ypres Tower Gun Garden

Rye Castle
Ypres Tower
Women's Tower & Medieval Garden

Built 900 years ago to defend the town, the Ypres Tower has been a fortification, a private home, a Court Hall and a prison. Now it's a Museum full of interesting objects spanning the history of Rye.

Together with the Women's Tower - one of the first prisons in the country built just for women - and a garden planted with Medieval herbs, they form the Rye Castle.

Open daily: April to October 10:30am to 5pm
November to March 10:30am to 3:30pm
Last entry 30 minutes before closing
Entrance charges apply · Children under 16 free with an adult

The Museum at 3 East Street is open weekends from April to October.
East Street free admission but donations encouraged

Rye Castle Museum

Office at 3 East Street, Rye, TN31 7JY
Phone: 01797 226 728 Email: info@ryemuseum.co.uk

The latest information is always on our website: **www.ryemuseum.co.uk**

Rye Heritage Centre Anchor

We hope you enjoy your visit or stay.

Best wishes

Rye Heritage Centre

CHAPTER 1

The Town of Rye

Here is an introduction to the sights you will see as you walk around the town.

Rye's history as a hill town has been heavily influenced by its geography and is remarkable for its struggles with the sea. Rye stands on fossil-bearing sandstone rocks and clays formed around 140 million years ago. Seen from a distance it looks like a pyramid. It was once an island surrounded by salt water.

Because the coastal edge here is made of shingle and sand, it is subject to powerful longshore drift movements of the waves. Laying within the area known as The Narrow Seas, between England and France, North Sea tidal surges can generate longshore drift to the east as well as the west of Rye. This made for hazardous navigation in medieval times to bypass the constantly evolving and moving giant shingle banks formed of pebbles and flints left over from the Ice Age melt. Exceptionally violent storms have hammered the landscape around Rye, as the climate was affected by the high-level dust-clouds from volcanoes across the world before 1300 in the build-up to the Little Ice Age.

Rye's relationship with the sea and the shingle are key to its past problems and eventual successful development. The sturdy and defiant character of the people of Rye has therefore evolved because of their ongoing struggles with sea and land. Rye has been a community with complex loyalties for and against the monarch of the time, and with internal rivalry between landowners and sailors, and external rivalry between ports and foreign powers.

Heritage photograph of a Rye fishing boat and its Skipper

In the days of King Edward the Confessor, Rye and Old Winchelsea were small fishing ports. In the second half of the 12th century they were invited into the Cinque Ports confederation as 'limbs' of the Head port of Hastings. Before he died in 1189, King Henry II gave these two limb ports the same privileges as the other confederation ports. These rights were confirmed by Royal Charter in 1278. In medieval times, the Antient town of Old Winchelsea was the dominant port in the area until 1287 when it was destroyed by a massive storm. The word 'Antient' is an early form of 'ancient'. This old word is derived from the French word 'ancien' meaning 'old'. Because of its proximity to the continent and the significance of its strategic location, Rye, along with New Winchelsea, was added to the Cinque Ports as an Antient Town in 1289. Later in the

14th century Rye and Winchelsea became full members of the Cinque Ports in their own right.

Once Old Winchelsea was covered by the waves, so Rye was ascendant until the well-meaning actions of landowners and farmers to enclose the salt marshes for good farming land caused Rye's harbour to silt up. In this constantly active and dangerous landscape, there has been a desperate struggle with the sea, to the point where, by 1600, authorities considered that the town might have to be abandoned as a port. A new harbour was to be built but that failed. Nevertheless, the indomitable spirit of the people of Rye and the profound respect that most English monarchs held for this member of the Cinque Ports, enabled new works to save the town.

Rye is now close to four rivers, the Brede, Pannell, Tillingham and Rother. The source of the Brede, twelve miles from the sea, is in springs emerging from the rocks around Netherfield, close to the town of Battle, famous for the Battle of Hastings fought between Anglo-Saxons and Normans on 14th October 1066. The Pannel rises near Guestling Thorn and flows past New Winchelsea. The Tillingham flows for twelve miles out of springs near Staplecross and the Rother, appropriately enough, stems from springs at Rotherfield and is thirty-five miles long. The history of all these rivers is complex, with riverbeds that have moved over time due to storms and silting, however, they all join as their waters flow southeast, finally flowing into the sea at Rye Bay via the main outlet of the Rother at Rye Harbour. Also in our beautiful and wildlife-rich landscape is the Royal Military Canal built to keep out Napoleonic troops.

If you stand on the long harbour arm at the mouth of the Rother in Rye Harbour and face France, thirty-two miles away across the English Channel (called La Manche in French), you will have the wonderful Rye Harbour Nature Reserve on your right. This stands on a great raft of shingle, called by geologists 'storm beach deposits'. On your left you will see the great sand dunes of Camber Sands and past them the Walland and Romney Marshes. Looking once again to your right down the coast towards Hastings, you will see New Winchelsea on its hilltop, and Winchelsea Beach and Pett Cliffs in the distance. Most of Old Winchelsea is under Rye Bay, destroyed by the sea in 1287, but some of it may be buried under the storm beach deposits near Castle Farm. Rye Bay is sometimes called Rye Camber. Camber is thought to come from the French 'chambrer' or bedroom, as a nautical joke, 'putting the ships to bed', being a large natural harbour, 'a safe haven'. This is where Camber Sands gets its name.

Looking to your left again you will be able to see the vast area of shingle that is Dungeness with its nuclear power station. This enormous shingle raft is the largest in Europe, another great wildlife area, in some circles accepted as the UK's only desert using the definition of an area which loses more moisture than it receives.

If you turn around and look inland, you will be gazing at Rye town and the High Weald, once a forest stretching across much of East Sussex and Kent, where the remarkable archer, William of Cassingham (now known as Kensham), nicknamed Willikin of the Weald, and his band of archer assassins inexorably hunted down the French Army of Dauphin Louis through the French invasion period of 1216-1217.

The beautiful Cinque Port of Rye

If you are staying even for a brief time, spare some of it to get out and about. Rye is connected by road, rail, coastal paths, and cycle tracks. For those looking for a relaxing but interesting holiday, there are many cafes, restaurants, delicatessen shops, art galleries, museums, bookshops, churches, and places to sit or stand and stare. Some world-famous parts of the town still have medieval street surfaces with cobbles, lined with old houses and inns. The Description of Historic Sites section at the start of this guide details the history of the oldest buildings.

Rye is a treasured jewel embedded in an active landscape, with close contact with fresh and sea water and wildlife habitats. Its natural activities have been to provide fishing resources, trade with the continent and the supply of ships to the monarch for coastal defence and warfighting. Some of its seaborne activities have involved piracy and privateering and there have been trials here for treason, heresy, and witchcraft. As we have mentioned, Rye is known as an 'Antient Town', part of the coastal defence organisation called the Cinque Ports. Nevertheless, it has been serially ravaged by the French, and the men of Rye have ravaged the coast of France in retaliation.

When the Cinque (Five) ports of Sandwich, Dover, Hythe, New Romney, and Hastings were joined by Rye and Winchelsea they became seven defence ports with their own court, known at first as 'The Shepway'. This Shepway Court was instituted so that the mayors of the seven ports together with officials called 'jurats' and 'bailiffs' could review policy, strategy, and capabilities. Representatives of the 'limb ports' who supplied extra ships and crews could also attend. Most importantly, these courts made decisions about how to meet the monarch's demands for Ship Service (building and providing war or transport ships) and how to remove misunderstandings between the ports. Later, the Shepway expanded to two courts called 'The Brodhull' meaning 'The Brotherhood', and the 'Guestling', named after the village near Hastings where this court first met. However, the courts could meet anywhere locally, and they often chose New Romney. These courts were ruled over at first by the Keeper of the King's Ships and they could rule on civil and criminal matters and had the power of life and death for offences of rape and murder. Exceptions involving matters of treason, heresy and witchcraft were referred to courts held in Rye with special additional powers granted by the monarch.

Rye was once a Borough but relinquished that status in 1974 when local government was widely reorganised. It now still has a mayor and town council and is part of the District of Rother. It has a fascinating and colourful history that is reflected in its buildings and institutions. This guide explains how the town has been a home to many refugees and religious communities, and how its history has been enriched by ceramics, art and literature. If you use this guide to walk through its streets, at every step you will surely sense the town's great history.

The following chapters will explore that remarkable history before we take you through past ages, dating the buildings you will see, their origin and purpose and linking them to the turbulent events that make up the character of Rye.

Augustine Chapel Steps on Conduit Hill

CHAPTER 2

After the Ice

The south coast of what was to become England was formed after the Ice ages. The great rivers now called Thames, Seine and Rhine all flowed into an embayment that was eventually to form the English Channel. England was still joined to Europe via Doggerland and by the Weald-Artois Ridge - a 21-mile-long chalk formation, one hundred feet high, that connected our white cliffs at Dover to those of Cap Griz Nez. When the ice melted a giant lake was formed in Scandinavia and eventually after thousands of years of pressure, the chalk ridge gave way with huge thundering waterfalls called the Fosses Dangard, eroding its chalk strata, and so the English Channel was finally complete. All the moraine material ground out by the glaciers, the flints and pebbles previously embedded in the ice, were thrust by the force of the water from the lake burst into the bed of the Channel where they now lie, to be used as shingle to protect our shores against sea level rises due to global warming. At this point, Rye was an island in a great bay of islands, including the island of Lydd.

Roman invasion

The Romans heard about the availability of iron for weapons, and they invaded in their great galleys. Eventually a huge iron production centre, the third largest in the whole Roman Empire, was formed at what is now called Beauport Park on the Iron Age Ridge trackway near Hastings (now the trackway is in Rother District). Here the Roman Navy's transport group called *Classis Britannia* had a villa (now destroyed) and a bathhouse fed by a small stream which remains deep in the woodland of the current park, on private property.

Later in the Roman period, the separation between Rye and the mainland of England lessened due to marshy conditions. So, in records dated to 428, there is a possible mention of Rye in the form of 'Riduna' (meaning 'ford'' or 'crosssing' in Latin), as being one of the forts controlled by the Roman Count of the Saxon Shore. Another 'Riduna' has been found in the Channel Island of Alderney.

Saxons from what was to become Germany raided our shores long before the Romans abandoned England to deal with troubles at home. The Romans appointed a Count of the Saxon Shore to make defensive forts including Pevensey Castle (Anderida). Once the Romans left, the Saxons invaded first around Selsey Bill and Pagham and moved to storm Pevensey, killing everyone and establishing a southern kingdom. After much fighting over territory, the Hastings and Rye areas were invaded by King Offa of Mercia in the period 770-772.

The Viking-Saxon Conflict

The Vikings came in repeated fleet attacks and then the great King Alfred took control of Wessex to repulse them using a series of coastal forts. Eventually the very first king of the whole of England was crowned. His name was Æthelstan (924-939). He was followed by a tumultuous set of kings that included Edmund I (939-946), Eadred (946-955), Eadwig (955-959), Edgar the Peaceful (959-975) and Edward the Martyr (975-978).

As you will read below, the next king was the inadequate monarch Æthelred the Unready who ruled first from 978-1013. At first, he battled against the Vikings, then, feeling overwhelmed, he paid them a vast fortune in Danegeld silver to leave our shores, but inevitably, they came back for more. The king fled to France and eventually the Danish Viking Sweyn Forkbeard (1013-1014) became King of England but died shortly afterwards so the nobles of the land called on Æthelred the

Unready to return and rule once more, which he did from 1014-1016. When he died, then Edmund Ironside, his son by Ælfgifu of York, his first wife, ruled during 1016 but lost England to the King of Norway and Denmark, the famous Viking, Cnut the Great (1016-1035).

King Canute as he is popularly called, married Emma of Normandy and this was very significant for the fate of Rye, so a detailed narrative is given below. When Cnut died, their sons, Harold Harefoot (1035-1040), Harthacnut (1040-1042) and finally Edward the Confessor (1042- 1060) ruled - making Edward almost the last Saxon King of England. But he left no offspring, so the throne was taken by King Harold Godwinsson, the Saxon-Danish warrior.

CHAPTER 3

The Great Transition

To understand the huge changes that Rye was about to undergo, we need first to look at what was going on far away in Eynsham, near Oxford.

It is thought that in the reign of King Edmund, he gave money and land to several women of royal descent to found nunneries. One such nunnery was at Wareham in Dorset and the Abbess there was named Wulfwynn. She had been gifted the land of Rameslie (Hrammesleagh in Early English) including Rye and in 982 she died, leaving her lands to her kinsman Aethelmaer of Eynsham in her Will. He was a leading subject of King Æthelred the Unready – (his dish-bearer or seneschal). In 1005, Aethelmaer founded Eynsham Abbey in Oxfordshire and donated Rameslie to it when he retired there. Eventually King Canute seized the abbey of Eynsham and so the Saxon Manor of Rameslie on the Sussex Coast, containing the Priory port of Hastings, the huge Rye Camber port and Old Winchelsea on its giant shingle bank, all passed into royal ownership.

There could hardly be a more important time for the fate of Rye than this period. As we mentioned in passing above, in a similar way to the Roman Saxon Shore defences, King Alfred established supply forts along the coast in a system called the Burghal Hideage and one of these is thought to be Rye. A great fleet of 250 Viking ships left Boulogne in 897. They were led by the fierce Viking, Haesten. They sailed past Old Winchelsea and Rye and up towards Newenden and on the way they massacred the farmers on the small hillock of Castle

Toll in the mouth of the Hexden Channel. They overwintered at Appledore and raided across southern England, deep into the interior. Eventually King Alfred managed to defeat them, and they left with depleted ranks.

During the days of the Saxon kings including the great Alfred, Rye, this well-positioned and growing fishing village on a hill in the marsh, was controlled by the Saxon manor of Rameslie. This consisted of both banks of the Priory Stream and its small harbour where Hastings Shopping Mall is now located and all the coast of Fairlight, Pett, Old Winchelsea and Rye. Then with almost endless attacks by Vikings, the status of Rye changed and in 1017 and, remarkably, for the next 230 years, Rye and the whole of Rameslie belonged to Normandy, not England. We could say that at the stroke of a quill pen on parchment, Rye was suddenly transported to what is now France. So how did this amazing change in rulers and land ownership come about?

As we have seen, King Æthelred II was King of England twice. His name means 'Wisely counselled', however because of his mistakes, to this was added (not in his lifetime) the Saxon word *unraed*, meaning poorly counselled. He therefore became known in modern popular literature as 'Ethelred the Unready'. During this first period of 'poorly counselled kingship', the land-hungry Vikings surged over England and settled. At one point the Vikings were paid 48,000 pounds of silver to leave. This might approximate now to one hundred million pounds.

Tired of paying Danegeld and deeply frustrated by his inability to keep his kingdom intact, King Æthelred ordered every Dane to be massacred on St Brice's Day, 13th November 1002. In that year, looking round for another dynastic marriage, he met and married Emma of Normandy.

At first, there were waves of Vikings crying for vengeance, but these were bought off once again with massive English silver tributes. Finally, the furious Danish king, Svein, aggrieved by the loss of his daughter as a consequence of the St Brice's Day Massacre, invaded England in 1013; Æthelred was unable to stop him. As mentioned above, Svein crowned himself king. Æthelred fled over the sea to Normandy, and the Christian monks of Fécamp Abbey sheltered the king until he was able to return upon the death of King Svein in 1014.

Although Svein's son Cnut the Great (King Canute) was hailed by the Vikings as the next king of England, the English Saxon nobles asked King Æthelred to return home from his refuge in Normandy, which he did, only to find that Cnut had a great army of Vikings to oppose his return. Remarkably, with the help of the King of Norway, the English king repulsed the Danish Cnut and drove him out of most of England. It was time to give thanks to God, but the fate of Rye was being decided.

As R. A. Vidler (1899-1991), the Rye historian points out, the Saxon lands of Rameslie Manor, held by the Church through Aelthemaer, the Saxon founder of Eynsham Abbey, were eventually given to Normandy. The Church wished to keep Rameslie and had this happened then there is no doubt that English history could have been very different. The 1066 Norman landings might have failed through lack of local support because Rye and Rameslie would not have been ruled by Normandy. But either wavering Æthelred changed his mind, or his manipulative second wife Emma of Normandy changed it for him, and there is even speculation that she may have lied about his intentions after his death. This was the crux for Rye. Queen Emma gave Rameslie to the Normans because, so she said, her first husband, the Unready King, wished to say thank you to the Normans for helping him when he fled. She convinced her second husband, King Canute, to give away Rye.

The grant of Rameslie to Normandy was one of the greatest ever mistakes in history. Why would we want to give away the key fishing, defence and transportation ports in southern England, not to mention their 100 salt pans, to the Normans? Nevertheless, some historians accept Queen Emma's allegation that in 1014 Æthelred II wanted the Saxon Manor of Rameslie to be given to Benedictine Abbey of Fécamp on the coast of Normandy, only 21 miles from Dover, to say thanks for sheltering him from Danish Viking attacks for many months. Was she a liar or had she promised her foolish former husband?

Thus in 1017, Rye on its sandstone and clay hill, and Winchelsea on its huge shingle bank in the Rye Camber Bay, with parts of the Hastings area including Guestling and Playden, became a province of Normandy. The citizens and religious persons of Rye were now answerable only to the Abbot and the Pope, not to the King of England. The fact that Rameslie was a Norman enclave had enormous implications for the future invasion of Duke William the Bastard. The monks, who naturally considered themselves Norman not English, were able to spy out the Saxon enemy for Duke William. These monks knew that King Harold had lands at Upper Wilting Farm near Crowhurst and a manor at Whatlington, near Sedlescombe. Both could be reached easily up the rivers and creeks by shallow draft longships and barges: Upper Wilting via Bulverhythe Harbour and the River Asten (now the Combe Haven) and Whatlington via the River Brede. So, for Duke William, the invasion and subsequent Battle of Hastings was just like coming home.

CHAPTER 4

The Norman Conquest

When Duke William's invasion began, two Norman longships veered off course and landed at Old Romney, south-east of Rye, only to find no Rameslie monks to welcome them but rather fierce Saxons who massacred the Norman crews.

When King Harold returned from his great victory against the Vikings at Stamford Bridge, having killed his own brother Tostig, he and his remaining brothers were killed at Senlac. Duke William remained on the battlefield until midnight, savouring his great victory, and during this time monks came to tell him of the massacre at Old Romney. Within the five days after the Battle of Hastings, Duke William had arranged for the respectful burial of his Norman dead and had given the Saxon corpses that had not been eaten by dogs and crows to the defeated Saxon families. He then moved along the coast and massacred the entire population of Old Romney in retaliation for their defence of the little port town before marching onwards to Canterbury.

1086 – Domesday Book

About the decision to send the king's officials into every town and village in England to compile the Domesday Book, a medieval writer says:

'He reigned over England, and so entirely did he understand it by his cunning policy, that there was not a hide of land within England that he knew not who owned it, or how much it was worth; and afterwards he put it down in his writing.'

So, what did the great Domesday tome say about Rye in Sussex? In 1086, the situation had changed somewhat, because not only was William the Conqueror now King of England but he was also still Duke of Normandy where Fécamp Abbey was located right next to the Ducal Palace. Consequently, there was more influence over the Abbot's activities. Rye was in the Rape of Hastings, in the Hundred of Guestling: A small part of Hastings, all of Rye, Winchelsea, Fairlight, Guestling village, Icklesham and Pett, and eventually Udimore, Brede, Beckley, Peasemarsh and Playden. It is important to remember that Domesday was a survey of manors, not towns, and so it does not mention Rye or Old Winchelsea by name.

The Domesday entry states:

'The ABBOT of Fécamp holds Rameslie of the king (William) and held it of King Edward. In the time of Edward, it was assessed at 20 hides but is now 17.5 hides.'

Mysteriously, it goes on to say –

'...In this manor is **a new borough**, and there are 64 burgesses paying 8 pounds and 14 bordars paying 63 shillings.'

Where could this new borough be? As the pagan Saxons, worshippers of Woden, were converted to Christianity, they built wooden churches at their location's highest or safest point. So modern historians claim this 'new borough is Rye'. It is believed that St Mary's Church, built on the highest point of Rye town, was re-established on its old Saxon site by the Abbot of Fécamp, called 'Little John' in 1085, one year before the Domesday visitation.

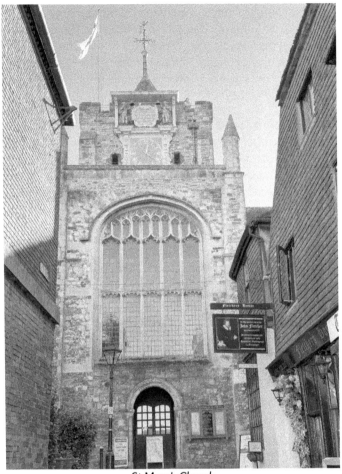

St Mary's Church

Finally, the Domesday book says:

'On this manor of Rameslie, Robert of Hastings holds 12.5 hides of the Abbot of Fécamp and Heoruwulf has half a hide. They themselves have 4 villans (villains) and 4 cottars and 2 ploughs.'

The 'five churches' mentioned in the Domesday Book are thought to be St Mary's Rye, two churches of St Thomas and St Giles on the island of Old Winchelsea, Brede Church and the Church of St Leonards, somewhere between Hastings and Brede. There was also a coastal forest call Dymsdale, now lost to the sea at Pett Level.

Now the Normans had settled in to rule the land. King William died in 1087 and his son William Rufus took over but was killed in the New Forest in 1100. Henry I then gained the throne, and so in 1103 plans were made 'for a church' in Rye – St Mary's. This must have been an enhancement to the existing church built in 1085 (see above).

By the time that St Mary's Church was established in Rye, Old Winchelsea was the dominant port of Rameslie, and it had a long-term relationship with Rye for trade and warfighting since they were both 'Antient Towns'. So here is a description of it from the book by David EP Dennis: *The History of Old Winchelsea*, on sale at Rye Heritage Centre:

'In the early part of the 13th century, Old Winchelsea was in its period of greatest prosperity. It had a large commercial capability, and its wide bay (now called Rye Bay) was the usual rendezvous for the English Fleet. More than once the French attacked it. To summarise its maximum development, we can say from charters and other sources written by historians that it had: Six thousand working people each day, seven hundred houses, fifty inns, a market, a cemetery, three churches, a monastery, a leper hospital, a causeway, several bridges, covered shipyards for two of the Winchelsea-style King's Ships, several boatyards, a fish dock, a herring salting factory, salt pans, two tide-mills, a prison, sea walls, a harbour arm, a ferry service, crops, cattle, and horses in stables. It had wine cellars in nearby cliffs. It had accommodation for meetings and for enabling the king and queen to sleep over in the town. Its vast harbour could hold at least one hundred ships. It was known all over Europe and was a constant source of trade with the continent – specially France, Spain, the area of Gascony and

Flanders. At one time one of its residents, the satanist Eustace the Monk, ruled the Channel Islands. It sent warships to Ireland, Wales, Scotland, France, Spain, and Portugal. It was the home of some of England's greatest pirates.'

CHAPTER 5

Rye and The Anarchy

Henry I died in 1135 and King Stephen ruled until 1154, however during this time there was war over the succession to the throne between Stephen and the Empress Matilda. During this period, called The Anarchy, the people of Rye in Sussex may well have experienced another nightmare like the hellish suffering during the reign of King Æthelred. To understand what life must have been like during the Anarchy, here are the shocking words recorded in the Anglo-Saxon Chronicle:

'Every chieftain made castles and held them against the king; and they filled the land full of castles. They viciously oppressed the poor men of the land with castle-building work; when the castles were made, then they filled the land with devils and evil men.   Then they seized those who had any goods, both by night and day, working men and women, and threw them into prison and tortured them for gold and silver with uncountable tortures, for never was there a martyr so tortured as these men were. One man they hung by his feet and filled his lungs with smoke. One was hung up by the thumbs and another by the head and had coats of mail hung on his feet. One they put a knotted cord about his head and twisted it so that it went into the brains ... I neither can nor may recount all the atrocities nor all the tortures that they did on the wretched men of this land.'

Death and famine followed, as the farms were depleted, and farmers murdered. If two or three riders came to a village, the monk said, everyone fled, for fear that they were robbers. Trade therefore came to a standstill, and those in want had no way to get supplies. Those travelling with money to purchase food would be robbed or killed along the way.

People began to say that 'there was no God'. The chronicler records that people said openly:

'Christ slept, along with His saints; he states that this — and more than we can say — we suffered 19 winters for our sins'.

Finally, in 1136 – King Stephen overwhelmed the forces of the Empress Matilda. Stephen died in 1154. King Henry II then ruled until 1189 and early in his reign, in 1141 Rye Mint, was founded and lasted until 1154 (but is not connected to the Mint House of today). In 1156 – Rye's famous Mermaid Inn was built. It was time to cheer up.

Rye's famous Mermaid Inn

Chapter 6

Rye's Crusades

We now enter the period of the Crusades. King Richard the Lionheart came to the throne in 1189 and ruled for ten years, during which time he was only in England for six months. He immediately began to use the ships of Rye to aid the recovery of Jerusalem. Ships from Rye and the other Cinque Ports accompanied the king to the Mediterranean where they fought Saladin's navy using reinforced wood and metal rams fixed to the front of their ships to impale enemy ships so that they could be boarded. No quarter was given, ordinary sailors and soldiers, often wearing heavy armour or chain mail stood no chance of survival. They were thrown into the sea to drown, although captured knights were usually held for ransom.

King Richard was held for ransom on his way back home and Rye was directly involved in his rescue. On leaving the Holy Land on 9 October 1192, Richard was on board a vessel, crossing the Mediterranean diagonally from the Levant coast, past Cyprus and Crete and on towards northern Greece. He was eventually forced by rough seas to dock at Corfu.

Fearing probable capture by Byzantine Emperor Isaac II Angelos (1155-1204), Richard dressed as a Knight Templar and sailed on from Corfu when the weather cleared, up the coast of the Adriatic Sea, only to be shipwrecked at Aquileia in the Friuli-Venezia Giulia region of north-east Italy. Having lost his ship, and failing to find another, the king began a long overland return to England. He was identified by troops of Leopold V of Austria (1157 – 31 December 1194) before he reached safety and was imprisoned in Durnstein castle in the Lower Austrian Wachau region on the Danube River. Since it was against the law to detain any holy crusader, Duke Leopold was excommunicated by Pope Celestine III (1106-1198).

In March 1193, Leopold forced King Richard to be passed into the hands of the Holy Roman Emperor Henry VI (1165-1197), whereupon Richard was locked up in Trifels Castle. Since the Emperor needed money to crush opposition to his rule in southern Italy, the capture of a king of England was a great gift. A ransom demand was made for 100,000 pounds of silver, which was around 2.5 times the total annual income of England. Since Richard's wife Queen Berengaria was still not in England, Richard's mother Eleanor of Aquitaine therefore implemented national taxation for all clergy and laymen.

After Henry's ambassadors, with a huge posse of knights and foot soldiers, conveyed the vast silver treasure to Henry, Richard was released on 4th February 1194, and he made his way to the coast. A fleet of ships left England to bring him home from Amsterdam. Within the flotilla was large ship from Rye in which he slept each night. A galley and a Rye ship were used to move the king along the coast of Europe and finally he came back to England to an impoverished citizenship. However, war payments and trade enriched Rye and in 1199, when King Richard died, Rye was being accused of 'being too rich to fight'.

CHAPTER 7

The Nightmare of King John

As soon as King Richard the Lionheart died, so a devil became king. This was John who ruled from 1199 to 1216. During his rule the people of Rye were in great danger from the invasion of the Dauphin (Prince) Louis of France.

Although King John attacked many people in England, he was good to the Cinque Ports. In 1202 he placed Dover Castle into the command of the powerful lord, Hugh de Burgh, but due to a failure of military campaigning, King John lost the whole of Normandy. He could see that he needed ships to fight the French, so in 1206 he gave an individual charter to each Cinque Port, developing their powers, giving greater scope to act in the realm's defence in 1212. This paid off with loyalty because as recorded in *Rotuli Litterarum Patentium* archives, King John and his court came to stay in Rye from Saturday 27th April until 1st May, and later in 1213 Rye's ship and crews did outstanding work to capture 200 French ships at the great Battle of Damme near Bruges. During this sea battle which took place on 30th and 31st May, King John was delighted to find that Rye ships had captured gold, silver, wine, bacon and other foodstuffs.

But because King John was so evil to many, the great barons of England, who had care of a little boy, the future King Henry III, decided to end John's rule by calling on the King of France and his son the Dauphin to invade. In 1216 the French invasion fleet arrived with thousands of troops and siege engines.

During the invasion, Rye ships with others of the Cinque Ports saved Dover Castle from being overwhelmed. Then King John died of dysentery. The boy who became King in 1216 when John died was Henry III. In 1217, Rye itself was captured by forces led by the satanist pirate Eustace the Monk, then the men of Rye recaptured their port. Dauphin Louis became King of England by acclamation of the barons only, because he had been excommunicated just in time by the pope. Eventually, the tables were turned, the rebel barons came over to the young king of England and there was a great victory by Cinque Ports ships at the Battle of Sandwich. Eustace the Monk, whose own battle cry was 'A Winchelsea!', had overloaded his ship with war weapons including a huge trebuchet, and many fully armoured knights. His wallowing flagship was boarded, and his head was chopped off by his former shipmate Stephen Crabbe of Winchelsea.

The Dauphin was paid a fortune to leave England and King Henry III finally received a full coronation. He soon gave Rye improved status and in 1219 Rye received permission to hold an Eyre. This was a circuit court headed by an itinerant judge on behalf of the king. The purpose was to settle disputes over land and powers. This was just in time for in 1221, the Constable of the Cinque Ports 'arrested' a consignment of wine following a riot. The Constable was the King's direct representative, and he was also the Admiral of the Cinque Ports. It was his responsibility to organise the defence of the coast and ports of southern England.

Rye was a key shipbuilding centre and in 1223 a royal order was made which forbade the export of timber via Rye because King Henry III was proposing to build more ships and galleys and the local woods were being used up for home cooking fires and home-building as well as exports to foreign countries.

In 1234, Rye and the other Cinque Ports had powers to control fishing and the sale of fish at Yarmouth, (now Great Yarmouth) and they often overtaxed or killed the people of Yarmouth, so in this year the king decided to investigate the brutalities against Yarmouth. At the same time, these increasing powers over Yarmouth and the trust put in Rye by the King led to a feeling that men could do anything they pleased. In 1235 Rye sailors were involved in piracy. They plundered the ships of foreign powers, killed the crews and took the spoils back to Rye. Sometimes this was done with the king turning a blind eye to the 'privateering' and sometimes the Rye and Old Winchelsea crews killed pilgrims and robbed them of the gifts they were bringing to the shrine of murdered Archbishop Thomas Becket at Canterbury.

Even so, war with France was looming once again and in 1237 the king told the Cinque Ports not to attack Bayonne in order to avoid further conflict with France. Between 1237 and 1243, the King's galleys were lying at Rye and Winchelsea and in the last year seven were laid up in Rye.

In 1241, Count Peter II de Savoy, known as 'The Little Charlemagne', was appointed as Keeper of the Coast, a title which eventually became Lord Warden of the Cinque Ports. He was a royal adviser to King Henry III, with powers to rule on shipwrecks and salvage, ship's pilots, trade and defence. In the next year 1242 King Henry III lost his battle against France and in vengeance he sent Rye ships to harry the French Coast and the French responded with their own raids on Sussex and Kent. A peace treaty was eventually signed in 1243.

Wine Cellar

Wine Cellar internal view

CHAPTER 8

No More Monkish Rule

We now come to 1247 – in this year, under the Charter of Resumption, the abbot of Fécamp finally lost control of Rye and almost all the whole of Rameslie. With the Pope's help, King Henry III gave Fécamp lands in Gloucestershire and Leicestershire in exchange for Rameslie which returned to English control except for a small area north of the town called now 'Rye Foreign'. The reason was, finally, that the king did not want French monks controlling the coast and banning the fighting of Normandy and France on religious grounds, when France was being so aggressive.

In fact, the king set out his reasons on 15th May 1247: 'for the better defence of my realm, it might be to conceal from foreigners the intelligence of affairs at home and stop them of such convenient ports of passage'.

Once Rye left the control of the Benedictine Abbot of Fécamp, so other orders of monks could come, and sure enough in 1248, the Augustine Friars came to Rye from Bologna, Italy.

The French were still a threat and so the idea of a castle for Rye came about when Prince Louis was invading England in 1216. It is thought that a small castle was built but destroyed later. King Henry III then gave permission for Ryers to build a new castle, at first known as Baddyngs Tower, and then as Ypres Tower. The town castle was built around 1241 to 1246 under the direction of Count Peter II of Savoy with the intention of a much bigger structure like Hastings, Dover or Pevensey Castles but the full works were not completed.

Rye had a strong partnership with Old Winchelsea, but this was ruined by storms. Between 1250 and 1287, the foundations of Old Winchelsea were gradually taken into the sea with great loss of life – and yet the survivors rebuilt repeatedly until it became impossible, and they called for the king's help. Repairs to the King's galleys were carried out at Rye in 1252 and again in 1253.

In 1250 Matthew Paris the chronicler said that:

'...the moon appeared swollen and red. Some churches, several bridges, mills, banks and three hundred houses were destroyed by the sea's rising waters. On that day, the tide was said to haven 'flowed in twice without ebbing, making a horrible noise' and at night the sea seemed to 'light a fire'. The large noble ships and some smaller craft were wrecked and foundered at a place called Hucheburne (early Eastbourne).'

The history chronicler Holinshead said:

'On the first day of October, a great tempest of wind such has hardly be known of or heard, caused the tide to flow twice without ebbing...and it struck fear into the hearts of those, dwelling far from the shore (on the island of Winchelsea).'

In 1251 there was a colossal increase in the height of the incoming tide, '...and it rose up six feet higher than it ever had done before, right on the equinox, overflowing its bounds, and causing injury to all on the coast.'

In 1252 the King's galleys were repaired at Rye once more because Old Winchelsea was being wrecked by the sea. The sea wall was fully breached, and the sea flowed right through the town once more. Full special rights for all the Cinque Ports were settled in law, but in this year, things got even worse.

The historian of the day, Matthew Paris, who may have been born in Winchelsea said:

'The great storm drove ships from their anchorages, raised roofs of houses many of which were thrown down, uprooted completely the large trees, deprived churches of their spires, made lead to move, and did great damage by land and still greater by sea, especially at the port of Winchelsea which is of such use to England and above all to the inhabitants of London. The east wind blew till it stirred up the south wind to visit this port of Winchelsea which is of great use to the English'.

In 1254 the King took sides in the Yarmouth Herring Fair disputes and was furious with Yarmouth, blaming them for fighting against the Cinque Ports. There was further bad news as the annual harvest of crops could not be gathered - it was covered in salt. The sea once again flowed right through Old Winchelsea town. The shingle spit was being taken away by spring tides combined with southerly gales. At the same time as the harvest was damaged and storms raged, there was worse news. In 1258 the French Earl Simon de Montfort raised a revolt against King Henry III and his son, Prince Edward. Montfort invited twenty-eight men from Rye to serve in his 'English Parliament'. Consequently, the people of Rye supported Simon de Montfort and his sons rather than the king.

Although the Cinque Ports had already been given individual charters, in this year 1260, for the first time, there was now one charter for the Cinque Ports as a whole. A 'Liberty' had been created. In 1263 the Friars of the Sack came to Rye and stayed until the order was dissolved in 1307.

On 14th May 1264, Simon de Montfort won a great victory at the Battle of Lewes. Rye's ships received payment for repairs from Simon in 1264, while King Henry III tried to bring the Cinque Ports into line. However, on 4th August 1265, Simon was speared through the neck with a lance and then castrated and chopped to pieces at the Battle of Evesham. Simon's son, also called Simon, arrived at the battle just in time to see his father's head hoisted on a pole, so he fled to become a pirate at Winchelsea and tried to raid London in retaliation for his father's castration. He then joined his brother Guy in Italy where, tragically, he and his brother murdered and mutilated their cousin, Henry Almain, King of the Romans. This assassination took place in Viterbo church during the Mass of the papal convocation. Henry had not been at Evesham, so was not guilty.

In 1270, to keep in the king's good books and get contracts to repair his ships the Ryers gave the king's son Edward a gift as he was on his way to the Eighth Crusade led by King Louis. At the same time, the friendly competitors of Rye and Old Winchelsea were once more in the front line of bad weather. The spire and part of the Old Winchelsea church of St Thomas was washed away in a storm, and so in 1272, an appeal for help was made to King Henry III that 'the sea is destroying Old Winchelsea town'. King Henry was too ill to go crusading and he died on 16th September 1272. The Cinque Ports gathered ships to bring the king's son back home from his crusade in 1273 as he was now the rightful King Edward I. Then, in 1282 ships from Rye sailed to Wales to support the new king's war campaign.

Mermaid Inn carriage entrance

CHAPTER 9

The End of Old Winchelsea and the Rise of Rye

Here we have the final destruction of Old Winchelsea port and town. On 4th February 1287, a roaring great tide came in and never ebbed. Everyone foolhardy enough to remain on what later became know as 'Vindelis' (A Latin name for Winchelsea caused by an Elizabethan map-printer's error) was killed. Nothing remained except a stone church steeple and after five more years that fell into the all-consuming sea. This is a severe lesson to us all as the coastline of Sussex is constantly challenged by the rising seas due to global warming. Millions of pounds are being spent on hundreds of thousands of tons of Swedish granite boulders to shore up our shores in 2024 and the endless movement of shingle by truck to save Dungeness Nuclear Power Station.

At length, a great inundation happened which submerged the marshy ground between Cliveden near Fairlight and Hythe. Winchelsea was no longer habitable. Many people climbed up the cliffs and watched in horror as a storm of unprecedented ferocity struck southern England. It was said to have made 'a pitiful waste of people, cattel and of houses in every place'.

A huge bolt of lightning struck the room where the King and Queen Eleanor of Castile were having a conversation and killed two of their servants. From the clifftop, the refugees from the storm could see that '...it carried off the poor folk below, piling people on cattle and on houses in a terrifying jumble' amongst giant waves, hurricanes, and shingle bank movements.

Some historians still maintain that the river Rother, previously meeting the sea at Lydd and later at Old Romney, was diverted by this giant storm to flow past Rye during the 1287 event. However, the historian Camden (1586) says this had already happened in 1236 and once more in 1250 but he also stated this again for 1287, and recent academic work has shown that the process of re-bedding of the river had been in progress for some time. We can therefore say that, over an extended period, the River Rother's normal course was blocked and so it changed course towards Rye where it flows today, leaving Old Romney bereft of a harbour.

While New Winchelsea was being built, in 1290 ships from Rye were supporting the king's attack on Scotland. At the same time, three years after the destruction of the shingle-bank town, the new Church of St Thomas was being built on the clifftop. A new harbour was developed with a ferry, and docks below the Petit Iham cliffs (Martin and Martin, 2004).

In 1290, the king granted that Rye could hold a fair and this gained the name 'Beggar's Bush'. However, there was no let-up in the war with France and in 1293 the king wanted to calm the situation and ordered the ports not to act aggressively to the French. The Cinque Ports took matters into their own hands, defying the King to force settlement of the problems in the Channel. A great Cinque Ports fleet was assembled which included Irish, Dutch, and Gascon ships fighting at sea against a fleet assembled by the Normandy, including Genoese and Flemish forces – a battle near La Rochelle which the Portsmen won decisively.

By 1294, as Rye headed into 150 years of attacks on France, Rye and other ports were controlled by Captains and in 1295, Gervase Alard of Rye was made Captain and Admiral of the Cinque Ports fleet, a matter of great pride to Rye. The elephant in the room was that his whole family were known pirates. The pride of Rye grew once more into aggression and as the king was being taken to France, ships from Yarmouth and the Cinque Ports were to escort him, but instead of proceeding peacefully, the Cinque Ports ships abandoned their mission and attacked the men of Yarmouth causing chaos. Things settled down once more and in 1299 – Rye ships were once again in Scotland with King Edward I.

CHAPTER 10

Fourteenth Century Rye

England needed money for its wars and so a customs tax was placed on wool exports in 1301. King Edward I died on 7th July 1307, and his successor was one of our most controversial monarchs. The new king Edward II spent a great deal of time learning how to thatch houses and dig ditches instead of fighting battles.

Cinque Ports piracy was becoming the norm and so a formal investigation was held into it by the state, but another inquiry into piracy had to be held once more in 1310, showing how hard it was to stop it. Ryers were no doubt pleased not to have to go to Scotland as the king ceased to attack it in 1323. However, in 1325, Rye ships took the queen on a diplomatic mission to France, and she refused to come back. Having turned against her husband she invaded England the next year and the king fled to Wales. He eventually gave up his crown and died, possibly murdered in a truly a horrible way, in Berkely Castle on 21st September 1327.

His crown went to their son Edward III and the new king called up Rye ships to take him to France, where on January 24th, 1328, he married Philippa of Hainault who was to give the king thirteen children in a happy marriage. In 1329 – payments called murage were taken to help defray cost of building Rye's defensive wall, including the Landgate.

It is thought that just before Edward III came to the throne, some nuns came to Rye from Assisi in Italy. They were of the Clarisses order formed in 1225 with St Clare as their patron saint. They are said to have built a chapel to their saint as a part of St

Mary's Church. In the chapel now is a stained-glass window with an image of Assisi which, being a hill town, looks very like Rye.

St Mary's Church Garden

The Austin Friars of Rye had been welcomed from Tuscany by Jew-hating King Henry III around 1248. By about 1330, Austins, the last big group of hermit monks to come from Italy to England had twenty-two houses in England and five in Ireland. By the time of the terrible Black Death (1348-49) there were around 500 Austin Friars in England. Women also lived as nuns under the Rule of St Augustine and by 1387 the number of Augustine English convents was between thirty-eight and forty-four. It is said locally that they brought silkworms with them and planted mulberry trees all over Rye, although no primary evidence of this local legend has been found. However, there is evidence of mulberry trees and silk production by the Huguenot refugees over the period 1572-1685. The Austin Friars built a monastery in Rye at the sea's edge – a big mistake because of storms and French attack.

The year 1337 was the start of the so-called 100 Years 'War' with France – even though we had been fighting on an off for many years before. It is inevitable the Cinque Ports ships would have conveyed troops for the Battle of Sluys in 1340 and Crecy in 1346. In the period 1346/7 there was the formidable Siege of Calais and then, a terrible blow came – The Black Death in 1348.

The Black Death, caused by the *Yersinia pestis* bacteria injected by fleabite gave people a truly wretched death with groin 'buboes', vomiting, ghastly headaches and swollen tongues. Those who were dying in agony found their skin developing black patches. This awful disease came to England from Gascony via a ship sailing into Weymouth in June 1348. Although the Romans had developed sewers and ways to remove waste, these techniques were soon forgotten. During the medieval period in Rye, a large wooden tower was built stretching out over the sea and from this was cast human waste.

The first major bubonic plague of 1348 led to the death of one third of the entire population of England (2 million) and one third of the population of Europe (25 million). In England, when the surviving peasants realised that they were desperately needed by the gentry to revive ruined agriculture, they asked for more money and this hatred and turbulence in society eventually led to the Peasant's Revolt of 1381. However, despite the appalling loss of life of 300 Rye citizens from the Black Death, the king still had to fight and so did the remaining sailors of Rye. Overall, Rye was fated to have hundreds of its citizens die of bubonic plague in the following years:1349, 1554, 1563 (562 died), 1579, 1590 and 1596.

Another glorious victory was achieved on 29th August 1350 when Admiral Carlos de la Cerda led the Castilian fleet into the Rye Camber with his ships loaded with treasure intended to pay for the defeat of England. Out sailed the men of the Cinque Ports in their fifty ships, with King Edward III and his son, the Black Prince on board. English naval forces headed into the Battle of Rye Bay, also known as Les Espagnols sur Mer. Cinque Ports vessels trounced the Castilians who had fourteen ships sunk. It is understood that Edward's queen may well have watched the battle from nearby Udimore ridge.

Because wool exports were being taxed there was a great temptation to smuggle it to foreign buyers. In 1359, a traitor is said to have let a force of three thousand French troops enter Winchelsea on a Sunday to give that population a taste of what Rye would experience in 1377. The 1359 attack was horrific, with troops 'killing all that withstood them, without regard to age, sex, degree or order'. They butchered the congregation attending Mass, smashed their way through the church and raped the women. There were so many dead that the church cemetery had to be expanded.

The Maritime History of Rye by John Collard explains that in 1360 a great honour was paid to the town, when King Edward III and the Black Prince landed at Rye on 18th May on their way back to London from the Reims Campaign. The king, his son and many English nobles backed by a huge field army of ten thousand men laid siege to the gates of Paris and this huge threat to the existence of France resulted in the Peace Treaty of Brétigny.

Mayors and Members of Parliament

In 1369 Rye had its first MPs in parliament. As related in the History of Parliament, most of the early mayors and MPs were pirates or self-seeking privateers. These were powerful men who did not pay many taxes because they were exempted through the laws of the Cinque Ports. William Long, one of England's most notorious pirates was a mayor and MP of Rye but also accused by the king of treason and multiple felonies. Many of these mayors and MPs were related to each other and formed a kind of 'Mafia' to get their own way.

Ypres Tower and River Rother

The Timeless Mermaid Inn

1930

2024

Discover 600 Years of History
31 Bedroom Hotel
2 AA Rosette Fine Dining Restaurant
Giants Fireplace Bar

 The Mermaid Inn

CHAPTER 11

The French Raid of 1377

King Edward III had titled himself (in what is called 'a pretence') King of England and of France, among other titles. After he died on 21st June 1377, King Richard II (called Richard of Bordeaux) came to the throne at the age of only ten years, with a regent to advise him called John of Gaunt. It was not until July 1377 that Richard had his coronation. In this period of English weakness, change and uncertainty, peace treaties were forgotten, and the French decided to strike. It seems that Rye was put on alert in 1376 but decided not to remove their goods and treasures from the town to places of safety and Winchelsea accused them of 'turning their back' to the French threat. This was a mistake.

A most severe attack was made upon Rye town and harbour on 29th June 1377. A large part of the French fleet of 120 ships plus 35 ships owned personally by the king of France and eight Castilian galleys commanded by Don Fernando Sanches de Tovar attacked Rye with around five thousand warriors and hundreds of sailors and rowers intent on destruction, rape and pillage. During the invasion, the town of Rye was burned to the ground, turning to ashes within five hours, women were serially raped, young girls were kidnapped, the Town Seal and the church bells were stolen from St Mary's. The church also lost all the lead from its roof. The four richest citizens of Rye were kidnapped, and 66 others were murdered in cold blood. This reveals the depth of the invasion. Later, some townsmen were hanged for a failure to resist. The French force then moved along the coast.

When Abbot Haimo of Battle Abbey heard about the terrible
destruction of Rye, he gathered some troops and rushed to New
Winchelsea on its hilltop where he led a magnificent defence
against a ferocious French raid with his monks in full armour.
When the French realised, they could not destroy Winchelsea
they went to Hastings but, finding nothing worth plundering,
they set fire to the town.

Not content with all this bloodshed and destruction, the French
and Castilian fleets sailed to the Isle of Wight, where Sir John
Arundel successfully defeated them. Then they moved to attack
Pevensey. There, the Earl of Salisbury drove them back to sea.
Quickly they turned towards what is now Brighton and attacked
Rottingdean causing the citizens to flee up into the tower of St
Margaret's Church. This was fatal because the French then set
fire to the church, and they all burned to death. In their fury,
the French then moved on to Lewes and set fire to the town and
several villages in the area. They captured and kidnapped the
Prior of Lewes Priory.

Presumably since King Henry III had taken Rameslie and
Rye away from Fécamp in 1247, local enmity developed over
one hundred years. Rye sailors engaged in constant piracy,
infuriating foreign powers. In the villages either side of Fécamp,
there seemed to be much hatred of Rye and records show
that Rye sailors identified two villages where the stolen bells
might be. The men of Rye and Winchelsea banded together
and raided the Normandy towns of St Pierre-en-Porte, a farming
village with huge limestone cliffs in the Pays de Caux region,
around 30 miles north-east of Le Havre and Veulettes, in early
1378, taking back the plunder, lead and bells. Veulettes, on the
River Durdent is around 27 miles southwest of Dieppe. During
these English raids on the French coast, hostages were taken.
It is known that the men of Rye set fire to St Pierre-en-Porte in
retribution. It seems they entered these ports at night and put
to the sword in a frenzy of bloody revenge everyone they met
who could not pay an immediate ransom.

In 1379, the predations of the sea and fear of further attacks by the French caused the Austin Friars to start building a new priory at la Haltone – now Conduit Street.

In 1381, England was in turmoil during the Peasant's Revolt. During this social turbulence, despite the temporary victory by the men of the Cinque Ports, the French then came back to Winchelsea with a better invasion plan and because the Earl of Arundel's defence was poor, Winchelsea was plundered. During this period, the French stole ships and wine and in 1382, a Rye ship, the Falco, and five other ships were recovered together with plundered goods and a whole cargo of wine.

In 1384, the situation in Rye and Winchelsea was raised with the king and Commons, both towns having been burned twice in two years. The resulting plea reveals the value of these two ports: 'Some remedy might be applied for the defence of the fortresses of Rye and Winchelsea which have so often been injured and almost destroyed by burnings and invasions of the enemy, because if those towns were taken, which God forbid, the whole country would be destroyed.'

The towns received full backing from the king and money to pay for repairs to walls and buildings. However, Winchelsea never recovered, and Rye became a more successful port. By 1385, the rivers around Rye were wide and flowing most of the time although silt was always a problem. Shallow draft ships and barges could easily reach the village of Bodiam, so Sir Richard Dalyngrigge built Bodiam Castle for a defence as well as a stately home.

During the period 1394 to 1405, Rye ships were hard at work taking King Richard II to Ireland and to meet the King of France, but the King, often physically unable to speak and thought at the time to be insane, was removed from the throne on 29th September 1399 and on 1st October of that year he handed his crown to Henry Bolingbroke, who became Henry IV.

Rye Town Seal - a replacement for the one destroyed in 1377

CHAPTER 12

Fifteenth Century Rye

In 1405, Rye ships took King Henry IV to Wales. After that, the town of Rye became caught up once again in war with France from 1413, when King Henry IV died on 14th March and a new monarch came to the throne one week later – the famous warrior King Henry V who would, within two years, win a great victory over the French at the Battle of Agincourt.

During this period the Royal Squadron, the ships of Rye and all the other Cinque Ports were employed in troop transport duties and coastal defence. Picture the scene as thousands of armed warriors, knights and archers came to the ports to be fed and sheltered until their ships were ready, then boarding and sailing in streams as the land army of England went to France. The taverns would be full, there would be loud cries in the marketplace as purveyors sold their wares. It was a time of great excitement; France would be defeated at last.

Once again, the king was concerned about piracy and in 1416, the law was changed to ensure that any piratical activity was equivalent to high treason. Because so many ships were needed during the Hundred Years War a special shipyard was developed in this period by William Caton, the Keeper of the King's ships who commenced building ships at Smallhythe, higher up the river Rother than Rye. Many Ryers were employed at Smallhythe, one of the most important shipbuilding locations in England.

A 120-ton clinker-built two-masted ship called a 'Ballinger' was ordered by King Henry V. Men such as carpenters and sailors would probably have travelled in Rye barges that plied to and fro on the rivers around Rye, reaching to Tenterden and Bodiam. However, when they reached Smallhythe, some of these workmen were further deployed to London Docks to work on exceptionally large ships that could not be launched from Smallhythe. These expert craftsmen had to walk to London docks, a distance of 44 miles.

In 1420, the remarkable King Henry V captured Paris and then the whole of Normandy. He became French Regent, generating a nationalistic feeling that nothing was impossible. In fact, almost the whole of France was now under the English yoke. The sailors of Rye would have been jubilant. Sadly, two years and several battles later, riding in full armour in the blistering summer heat, he had heatstroke followed by dysentery. The great hero of England, Henry V died on 31st August 1422 at Bois de Vincennes. His body was brought back from France, accompanied by the Cinque Ports ships. The jubilation at Rye would have turned to the deepest sorrow as their hero, who was almost ready to be crowned as King of France, was taken from them, leaving Charles VI (Charles the Mad) to become French king, only to die two months later.

This became even more of a sorry mess when Henry V's nine-month-old son Henry VI came to the throne on 1st September 1422 after Charles VI died. Later, King Henry VI was seen to act in an eccentric way which turned into madness. Nevertheless, on 27th July 1437 a remarkable Royal document came to Rye. It said that King Henry VI had given his Royal Pardon to everyone in Rye for any crime committed prior to the 2nd September 1422 (the day after the king's accession). The categories of crimes that were forgiven tell us a great deal about Rye's unruly society. They were, in order of the king's concern for them: prophesying, murder, rape, rebellion, insurrection, felony, conspiracy, neglect, extortion, imprisonment, contempt and errors, concealment, deception, counterfeiting and coin clipping, and stealing timber.

All these pardons were given in thanks for the people of Rye who in the reign of King Henry V had found war materiel and defences and courageously attacked the French town of Harfleur, other parts of Normandy and the castle of Calais. Even so, people were unhappy with their lives. Just as trouble was brewing in 1449 because of the corruption of those who were advising the king, so Tenterden became a limb of the Cinque Port of Rye.

In 1450, despite his mental incapacity, Henry VI (1422-61) still ruled England and people were aware that he appeared simple-minded. Rye, the whole of the Cinque Ports and almost all of England must have become fearful because of the king's ongoing strange behaviour. The king was seen playing with a live bird attached by string to a stick that he waved about.

When France was lost in 1453, then English soldiers coming back through Rye and the other Cinque Ports were paid to join private armies of regional lords. However, in 1475, Rye and other Cinque Ports vessels were called to transport troops for a massive invasion of France. The new king Edward IV wanted to prove that he was still technically the rightful King of France despite English losses. Even though the French had a bigger army, they gave in when the ships of Rye and other ports sailed into Calais and the onboard troops penetrated into France. Another treaty was then signed – called Picquigny (Somme).

King Edward IV died on 9th April 1483 and his successor was Edward V, a little Prince, who it is traditionally said, was smothered with pillows along with his brother the Duke of York, in the Tower of London in July 1483, seemingly on the orders of the eventual monarch Richard III.

Child murderer or not, Richard III honoured the Cinque Ports at his and his Queen Consort Anne's coronation on 6th July 1483. He asked the Barons to carry the silk canopy over the royal couple and for the Mayor and jurats to bear four spears and four silver bells, which they brought back to Rye in perpetuity. This tradition has been carried on over the centuries and

Rye's Mayor was most recently included in the party for the coronation of King Charles III.

This notorious king, Richard III died on 22nd August 1485, killed at the Battle of Bosworth Field. His body was found during car park excavations in Leicester in 2021. Then King Henry VII known as Henry Tudor came to the throne. On 21 April 1509 he died, and Henry VIII came to the throne. So, in the tumultuous space of 26 years, England had four kings.

CHAPTER 13

Rye's Tudor Nightmare

We now relate the history of Rye during the reign of King Henry VIII. Key characters are Robert Wymond, William Inold and Randal Bell. What happened to them reveals the awful pressure that Ryers were under that led to some taking life-threatening risks in a saga of treason, heresy, and witchcraft.

In Rye as elsewhere in the kingdom, King Henry VIII's reign was a time of fear and death in which the very worst behaviour of humanity came through as people spied and reported on things that were matters of air rather than substance. In our scientific days we do not give much credence to witchcraft, scrying and necromancy. Heresy can easily be overcome by swapping church communities in a pick-and-mix kind of way, so that the heretical thoughts you had in one place were now *de rigeur* in your new religion. Witchcraft is no longer illegal and only treason remains.

The Advent of King Henry VIII

Henry was born on 28th June 1491 and came to the throne on 24th June 1509 after the first Tudor, Henry VII died. In 1512, worried about invasion from France, he ordered the building of a castle at Camber near Rye although work was slow and expensive mistakes were made in its construction. As is well known, he then began a series of marriages, divorces, and executions with the aim of brutally removing anyone who stood in his way of providing a lawful son to succeed him. Another aim was to ensure that he dictated what was acceptable belief, not the Pope in Rome.

Camber Castle

The title "Defender of the Faith" was first conferred by Pope
Leo X on King Henry VIII on October 11, 1521, as a reward for
the king's pamphlet "*Assertio septem sacramentorum adversus
Martinum Lutherum*" ("*Declaration of the Seven Sacraments
Against Martin Luther*"). However, when he found that Pope
Clement VII would not bend to his demands, he schismatically
separated the new Church of England from the Roman
Catholic Church, leaving everyone to choose between death
and capitulation. As a result, he and his chancellor Thomas
Cromwell ensured that a great many people would die terrible
deaths if they did not bend to the Royal Will. Rye was directly
affected by these new laws and English parliamentary papers
show that Thomas Cromwell was watching the piratical people
of Rye like a hawk.

Henry was concerned about French intentions and so he
ordered the enlargement of castle fortifications at Rye Camber
and the next year the Cinque Ports conveyed his troops
to France. The year 1535 marked the commencement of the

Dissolution of the Monasteries. In 1536, King Henry VIII's Ten Articles of Faith were published, and this affected Rye directly too. The concept of food and drink becoming body and blood stems from the Christian Bible's New Testament text concerning the Last Supper in which Jesus Christ institutes the Lord's Supper aspects of Body and Blood. Matthew, Mark, Luke, and Corinthians all mention the incident of breaking bread and drinking wine. John does not describe the Eucharist in such a detailed way but instead his references to that concept of Body and Blood are more mystical and allegorical.

There was no stopping Henry. In 1536, the *Ten Articles of Faith* were now law. Everyone in Rye had to decide on pain of death: Do I think the body of Jesus is inside the Host and Wine at the moment of elevation in the Mass, or not - and do I think my soul might go to Purgatory or not?

Rye was deeply divided between Catholic and Protestant as we shall now see in the next chapter.

St Mary's Church at the apex of Rye

CHAPTER 14

No More Monasteries

The stress of the Reformation and the deeply controversial
marriage of the king to Anne Boleyn began to expose cracks
in the good order of the state. At some date during the
physical processes of the Dissolution of the Monasteries
- 1536-1541, a brave (or foolhardy) Austin Friar of Rye was
named as 'Friar Sir James' by Cinque Ports Lord Warden Sir
Edward Guildford in a letter to Henry VIII's chancellor, the
notorious Thomas Cromwell. Friar James had openly opposed
the religious changes under Henry VIII. This friar was arrested
by the Mayor of Rye and put in Guildford's custody after having
spoken seditiously against the King's new marriage to Anne
Boleyn on 1st June 1533. The powerful courtier Sir Edward had
been Marshal of Calais back in 1519 and was the king's Master
of the Armoury for life.

The mayor and jurats of Rye had special status as they were the
powers of the Cinque Ports and so they reported to Cromwell
on 8th June that two local investigators, Alexander Wellys and
John Raynolde, had searched the home of Rye's curate William
Inold and found certain books and bills. At least one of these
books advocated the maintenance of a church led by a pope
and not by a king of England and their discovery caused William
Inold to be taken away from the parish of Rye and imprisoned
on the specific orders of Thomas Cromwell as Protestantism
rolled into Rye on the crest of a wave.

Gillian Draper, in her book on the history of Rye says:

'The religious controversies which affected the town and its
government from as early as the 1520s made the church building
a controversial space. Annual civic and religious rituals, such
as the celebration of the feasts of St Anne, the Transfiguration
and the Holy Name of Jesus, were held in the church and
churchyard in the 1530s under the influence of the traditionalist
curate, William Inold, until he was removed and imprisoned.
The celebrations were opposed by a vigorous faction among the
town government led Thomas Birchett (II), who was the town's
first Protestant MP in 1539. Birchett's position was consolidated
by his appointment as mayor in 1545, under the influence of
Cromwell, and its confirmation under Edward VI in 1548.'

The Sacramental Treason of Randall Bell – August 1539

The Rye priest Inold plainly did not accept the kingship of Henry
VIII and there were still many Rye people, perhaps in real shock,
who would not comply with the king. One of these was Randal
Bell. He was a hatter and capper who traded in the Cinque port
town of Rye and the administrative town of Lewes. After the
king's signing of the Six Articles in June 1539 and the expulsion
of priestly families in July, in August 1539, Randall Bell decided
to act.

He attended Holy Mass at St Mary's Church and took with him
his dagger. He was wearing his trade token, his cap, upon his
head. As soon as the host or sacred circular token of bread was
raised in that sacramental moment, he rushed to the altar rail
and tried to snatch the host from the elevating hand of the new
parish priest, calling out:

'Thou art a false knave. Thou cannot not make God.'

Seeing the dagger, a member of the congregation, Robert
Wymond, a jurat of Rye, bravely tackled him, and presumably
with other help, 'commanded him to prison' where he was
rigorously interrogated.

Here is what else Bell said under interrogation so that readers can see how violently opposed to King Henry VIII's *Six Articles* he was, in the specific case of transubstantiation. The likely prison in those days in Rye was the Ypres Tower (formerly known as Baddyngs Tower). Because the allegations were so serious, Randall Bell's interrogation was recorded in the paper file of the Special Commission appointed to take over from the normal Cinque Ports courts. This page-stitched file is held by the East Sussex and Brighton and Hove Record Office (ESBHRO).

The interrogation can be interpreted like this:

Interrogator: Why have you done this thing – speaking out against your king?

Bell: Of my own courage I have come up to the altar here in Rye with the intent of saying that the sacrament is nought. Not only that but I can tell you that I have been commanded to do that by the King's own Council.

Interrogator: Whom do you mean? Who is the King's Council to your mind?

Bell: Why, the Earl of Shrewsbury - and also the Lord Montacute, of course!

Interrogator: How can you justify this?

Bell: I will justify it by telling you that the Church stands awry. The Church is not as Christ did leave it.

Interrogator: Why tell you this?

Bell: Because Christ is removed - in that the Pope is refused to be the head of the church (by the king's usurpation) and therefore there can be no salvation, nor any due administration of the Sacraments.

Interrogator: What would you then do?

Bell: If I could have caught the sacrament, I would have trodden it under foot. I would have cast the chalice into the middle of the Channel.

Interrogator: The King's law is the law. How can you offend against it? What reason do you have?

Bell: My reason is plain – it is that the king is your king and not my king. Understand that I, Randall Bell have more right to the crown than the king.

Interrogator: Have you said anything like this before?

Bell: I have informed the king's council the last time I was in prison in Rye.

Although there is nothing in these documents to prove that Bell was executed by burning, it is hard to understand how he could have escaped the justice of the time because he had no right of appeal and no justification in law, nor could he recant. He was surely doomed. Certainly, 27 men were called as potential jurists judging him and of these 12 were sworn in on 13th September 1539. However, it is interesting that Bell claimed that Shrewsbury and Montacute told him to seize the host because, George Talbot, 4th Earl of Shrewsbury was loyal to King Henry and saved him from defeat during the Pilgrimage of Grace riots in 1536 - but Henry Pole, 1st Baron Montacute, justice of the peace for Sussex, was executed for treason on 9th January 1539.

There is also more mystery - just why was Bell in Rye prison on a previous occasion? In the Chamberlain's accounts for this matter, there is an entry explaining that a charged fee is for a letter to the bishop setting out 'the demeanour of the traitor.' Then there is a charge for 'conveying the traitor to the Council'.

St Mary's Church Altar

The Resurrection of William Inold

In 1537, the removed Rye priest, Inold, had talked himself
out of arrest and with vengeance in his heart he had been
investigating the activities of Rye's MPs and their friends.

Inold quickly turned the tables on jurat Wymond and his clique
of Rye and parliamentary friends including William Mede, and
Alexander Welles (who had searched his house), his co-MP in
parliament and accused the group of treason against the king.

Following the *Act of Supremacy* in 1534, the monastery
community was then dissolved in 1538 and the monastery fell
into disrepair, but the Austin Chapel remained as a useful
building and is still in Rye today.

The History Jar sums up the story of William Inold:

'William Inold, the vicar of Rye, had already got away with
offending the king once. In 1533 he had likened Henry VIII's
actions to those of King John when the medieval monarch
had managed to incur papal wrath and get himself and the
whole country excommunicated. Cromwell had Inold arrested
on account of his seditious sermonizing, but he was eventually
released. The new treason laws of 1534 ensured the vicar did not
escape a second time and the letter in the archives suggests
that the evidence collected by Cromwell for the vicar's second
trial was guaranteed to ensure an unhappy end for Inold.'

However, this is just not true as you will read below. There was
no unhappy end. The state archives entry really means that
curate Inold became the Vicar of Rye in 1541 when the so-called
missing vicar died.

By now, if Thomas Cromwell had lived, then curate Inold would
have been burned. But he is about to reappear. Robert Wymond
attended parliament in 1545 as one of Rye's MPs along with
Alexander Welles. The last use of Camber Castle to engage with
the French is also in this year as the Castle usage was gradually
lost due to silting.

The Death of King Henry VIII

King Henry could sense that he was going to die because on 30th December 1546 he drew up his Will, asking to be buried in the Choir of the College of Windsor 'in an honourable tomb for our bones to rest in'. The Six Articles were repealed by the Treason Act signed by Jayne Seymour's Protestant son, King Edward VI, who was crowned on 20th February 1547.

There is proof that despite any tainting by Inold, Wymond and his fellow MP attended parliament in 1545. Wymond survived his king. He was still MP for Rye in 1548 and he was re-elected as a Rye jurat on 26th August 1548. Then, becoming ill, he made his will on 27th May 1549 and died prior to 24th September 1549.

The Last Laugh

Though we might think that Inold should have been executed for treason, you cannot keep a good man down and sure enough the Chichester Diocese records show that he survived at least to 1544.

So Inold outlived Thomas Cromwell. As he stood outside the beautiful church of St Mary's looking towards the bastions of the Ypres Tower, the ships on the river Rother and the sparkling sea of Rye Camber, how he must have laughed.

Inold stuck to his traditional Catholic beliefs, never giving in to the emerging current of Protestantism He did not recant or beg and yet he opposed the king and his formidable chancellor.

Sadly, St Mary's Church became neglected by the Protestants. They stripped out much of its glory. Gillian Draper says in her History of Rye:

'Between 1546 and 1548 the churchwardens and the new staunchly Protestant vicar, Edmund Scrambler, enthusiastically removed the rood loft and three tables next to the high altar on which certain 'idolles' stood. The early triumph of the Protestant members of the town structure appears to have been two pillars at the sides of the door into the north transept. After the Reformation, the two chapels (the south and north chancels) were separated from the rest of the church and put partly to secular purposes. The north chancel was used for storage, including perhaps for smuggled goods, although burials continued to be made there in the eighteenth century. The south chancel was used for guns and stores from 1585 and in 1637 a complaint was made that it was used as prison and for the execution of punishments. It was later divided into two floors, and the upper one was used as a school for poor pupils.'

In 1544 the plague returned to Rye with 436 fatalities, nearly twenty percent of the population. Because King Edward VI was a young boy, born 12th October 1537, he had courtiers vying to look after his interests. One of these was Edward Seymour, 1st Duke of Somerset who was appointed Lord Protector of England from 1547 to 1549. In the middle of this period, 1548, he visited Rye, however, due to the unpopularity of his governing methods, he was arrested and placed in the Tower of London where he was decapitated on 22nd January 1552. It may be that the reason for his visit to Rye was the growing concern that the dumping of ship's ballast was now so great that combined with the draining of the marshes, the flow of water into the Rother was weakened to the point where the watercourse was full of stone and silt. Anyone seen dumping ballast was to be fined £2.00 (£914.00 in 2024).

In 1556 plague came back to Rye once more and then, beginning in 1566 the refugee Sea Beggars and Huguenots arrived.

The famous cobbled streets of Rye

CHAPTER **15**

Rye and Queen Elizabeth I

The wonderful buildings in Church Square

When Queen Mary I died on 17th November 1558 of suspected uterine cancer, then the daughter of Queen Anne Boleyn and King Henry VIII, Queen Elizabeth I was crowned in Westminster Abbey on 15th January 1559.

In this period, the Spanish ruled the Netherlands. Opposition grew in 1566 when members of the Netherlands nobility, followers of the religious preacher Calvin decided to try and take back their country from Spain. To do so they formed a colony of ships called the Sea Beggars, (WaterGuezen) using Rye and other Cinque Ports harbours as a refuge against Spanish attacks.

In this terrifying religious and political seesawing, Rye had moved towards Protestantism under Henry VIII, then back to Catholic practices under Mary I, and now back to being protestant under Elizabeth's rule. This period was a frantically busy one for Rye, despite legal restrictions on the use of timber for furnaces and the silting up of the harbour year by year, Rye was still in great demand.

In 1561 an interesting case of witchcraft occurred in which 'Mother Margery' was thrown out of the Rye Alms-houses for 'notorious offences' in which she kept a complete side of beef to go rotten for the purpose of making curses.

The continental surge of Protestantism caused a revolution in part of France and protestant reformers looted the city and Roman Catholic churches of Le Havre. Instead of sitting and waiting for doom in the shape of the French Royal Army they called upon Queen Elizabeth I of England and she immediately saw there was a chance of getting Calais back after its capture by the French in the war of 1557-1559.

Elizabeth signed the secret Treaty of Richmond in 1562 with the leader of the Huguenots, Louis, Prince of Condé and she confirmed that three thousand troops would be sent via the Cinque Ports to take Le Havre and Dieppe. Sure enough the ships of Rye complied and the English troops started to build fortifications in France. However, the French army then attacked and expelled them so they had to be rescued by our stalwart Rye ships once more.

St Mary's Church records show that in the period 1561-2, Lewys Billiard was a French Huguenot refugee who settled at first in Winchelsea. He then moved to Westminster where he was employed by the Royal clockmaker to Queen Elizabeth I. He fitted a new clock to St Mary's Rye to replace on older one installed in 1513 that had ceased to keep time. Some horological historians think that Billiard did not make the clock himself, despite several recent books claiming that he was its inventor. Instead, he assembled it from pre-existing parts that may have been meant for another church, monastery or cathedral. There is even a speculation that it may have come from Hampton Court Palace. You can read more about this remarkable and controversial timepiece and its mysterious history in the Guide section titled: Description of Historic Sites.

Rye was still suffering. To make matters worse, the plague returned in 1563, killing 779 people – one third of Rye's population. By 1565, Rye's population was estimated at 2,468 with 1,600 being women and children, leaving only 868 men to build and man the ships, defend the coast, and keep the farms going. Compare this with the current (2021) population of 4,975. In 1571, the Tillingham sea wall burst again and in 1572, John Prowze drew a detailed map of Rye harbour and town.

Religious persecutions and massacres of the Huguenots were in full flow. They were French and Flemish-Walloon Protestants of the Reformed Church of France. Understandably this caused many to flee to the ancient Cinque Ports towns of Rye and Winchelsea. They arrived on boats from 1562 onwards after the Massacre of Vassy on 1st March 1562 and eventually there were one thousand five hundred refugees living in Rye, representing 42% of the local population. Some were housed in the Chapel of the abandoned Austin Friary.

In 1572, Queen Elizabeth I suddenly refused to admit the Sea Beggars to her harbours, the strategy being to force them out to attack Spain and thus help the Dutch. In the same year, the population of Huguenots in France reached two million; they were hated by the Roman Catholics who began to kill these Calvinistic protestants in Paris and across the countryside. People, including children and babies were executed by defenestration, mutilation, disemboweling, mass drowning in the Seine and whatever other cruel deaths could be conjured. Twenty-five thousand Huguenots were killed in Paris

in the St Bartholomew's Day Massacre and about another seven
thousand in the countryside by 17th September.

*St Mary's Church Clock and
Quarter Boys*

In 1573 Queen Elizabeth I left London and came to nearby
Northiam, where she sat under an oak tree on Northiam Green
for a lunch feast and left a pair of shoes that are still conserved
today. When the Queen changed shoes, the pair no longer
needed were given to Mrs Frewen at Guldeford Lodge, Rye.
The queen arrived at Rye on 11th August via the Postern
Gate, bringing her whole Court from London. She stayed for
three days, consuming water from Rye's Blykwelle, now called
Queenswell. She liked the town which at the time was the most
important port in Sussex. She stayed locally and awarded the
town the accolade 'Rye Royal'. At this time, an estimate was
made that the recovered population of Rye was five thousand
plus refugees but less those trading across England or working
at sea.

Rye was growing and now in 1576 there were forty public houses
where people mixed. This may have led to easy access for the

bubonic plague which came in 1577 and 1579, then in 1580; 813 people died of it.

In this year, it was realised that the increase in local manufacturing of glass and iron goods, required the diversion of river water to the mills and furnaces and also excessive use of wood to heat the metal and glass. So the villages of Westfield, Brede, Guestling, Northiam, Beckley, the whole of the Isle of Oxney, Iden and Woodchurch were instructed to desist from taking river water for their 'iron hammers', using water diversion gates, because 'by cutting a gate, the water is turned from its accustomed course to the Channel and so runs to the mill of the said iron hammer'.

Then Rye started to decline dangerously, and this could be seen by the types of crimes that were being judged in the Cinque Ports Courts as people tried to find ways to make money and stay alive.

Between 1583 and 1587, people were accused of 'stealing the mainsails from a ship', selling candles in the countryside when the people of Rye needed them, selling candles to the French and refusing them to Ryers, and keeping pigs inside the town walls, also selling bread that was underweight, walking at night and attacking people – and amusingly, 'being a scold so loud that people could hear her far off'.

In 1594, Symondson's Maps of Rye Harbour (now hanging in Rye Town Hall) and Romney Marsh were drawn up.

In the late 1590s the Anglo-Spanish War was in full swing, and it became vital to capture the great Spanish port of Cadiz. Sir Roger Devereux, 2nd Earl of Essex and Admiral Charles Howard led a huge fleet of English and Dutch ships and warriors. They swept in almost unopposed. Because of the opposition in Holland, the failure of the Spanish Armada and the loss of Cadiz, Spain declared bankruptcy in 1597.

Queen Elizabeth decided to send an expedition from Rye to totally destroy the Spanish fleet and capture the Azores.

This was the Islands Voyage campaign in June to August 1597. Although the Azores could not be captured, the great treasure ship of Spain, Madre de Deus, was taken with all its gold; it is said to be one the largest and richest ships ever to be taken by our navy.

CHAPTER 16

Desperate Measures to Save the Harbour

With the destruction of Old Winchelsea in 1287 and the decline of New Winchelsea in 1550, all was set fair for Rye to be the dominant port of the area, except for one thing – it was losing its harbour. This was due to multiple causes. To ensure the stability of ships that had delivered their goods to English or foreign ports, stony ballast was placed in the holds to act as a gravity weight. There was a tradition of dumping ballast into harbours from cargo-empty ships so that they could load new cargo. Farmers continued to take land from the sea reducing the cleansing effects of flash flooding of streams. The longshore drift was still casting large shingle banks along the coast. The silt from the four rivers surrounding Rye was leading to the harbour's almost total suffocation. Something had to be done.

As we have seen, in 1573 – on 11th August Queen Elizabeth I visited Rye but even in this year of royal accolades there were bitter fights between Rye landowners and sailors over land grabs and harbour silting. Consequently Rye only managed to supply one ship and around fifty sailors to help to defeat the Spanish Armada in 1588. It was obvious to the monarch that Rye and Winchelsea shipping facilities were an essential part of the defence of the realm and its trading capability and so in 1593 the Italian engineer Frederico Genebelli was asked to conceive a plan to save Rye harbour.

The project to renew Rye Harbour was also intended to provide a solution to the terrible state of Winchelsea harbour by cutting through the marshes at the back of Winchelsea to reach the sea at what is now called Smeaton's Lane, Winchelsea Beach, where the harbour area has been preserved as an open green space. The joint project was originally Genebelli's but later an English surveyor and engineer called Smeaton, who had built the Eddystone Lighthouse, became minimally involved some thirty years after the project began. Strangely therefore, the project is now known by the name of 'Smeaton's Harbour'. Through no fault of Smeaton's, this was a disastrous, ineffective, and expensive fiasco.

In 1603 James VI of Scotland who had been crowned there in 1567, was then crowned James I of England (1566-1625). He, as King of Scotland, already had a deep interest in witchcraft. He considered it part of the theology of religion.

King James was so impressed with witchery that he took part in torturing women accused of witchcraft and then wrote his book *Daemonologie* in 1597 and this was used by William Shakespeare to write part of Macbeth.

Now he was King of England, in 1604 he ordered the publication of a new Witchcraft Act. In the days of Elizabeth I, witchcraft did not include conjuring spirits to help search for buried treasure, but it was, nevertheless, a capital felony meaning death if anyone was killed due to witchcraft. However now that King James was on the throne, even searching for treasure was considered to be witchcraft if it was known that the perpetrator was dealing with evil spirits for any reason. This brings us back to Rye.

In 1603, George Taylor's wife died, and he married Anne Bennett. She was drawn into the world of witchcraft by the Swaffer family who, in 1607, moved to Rye. The mayor of Rye Thomas Hamon's wife Catherine died, and he married Martha Tharpe. By the midsummer of 1607, Susan Swaffer was seeing spirits looking in through the window of her home. Then the Mayor of Rye died and Martha Tharpe, now Hamon, married the new mayor, Thomas Higgons. More apparitions were seen on 15th September. Had Anne and Susan used witchcraft to murder the Mayor of Rye? By 26th September, Susan Swaffer was taken to be interrogated by magistrates, but Anne fled to Kent. During October and December, the trial was proposed but due to a legal technicality it was challenged by local lawyers and by the Lord Warden of the Cinque Ports in the period 1608-9. Later Anne was captured and in 1608 she refused to plead which would normally have meant that she would be crushed between rocks until dead (pressed to death). In the June of 1609, more evidence of witchcraft came to light, but Anne was acquitted, and by 1610, Susan was pardoned.

There were repairs to be done to the town and its surrounds and despite James I's interest in torturing and killing witches, he was also keen to save Rye's landscape, so on 27th June 1604 he had set up a commission to look at the way that water was channeled and drained in Rye and across the whole of Romney Marsh. This commission had some mighty men in it including the Earl of Dorset, Lord High Treasurer of England and the Earl of Northampton, Lord Warden of the Cinque Ports. The commission was instructed to examine and repair all the water channels, gutters, rivers, streams, banks, walls, and channels to stop the rainstorms and relentless sea from ruining the landscape. This work was to cover a vast area including Appledore, Newenden, Robertsbridge, Rye, Udimore and Peasemarsh. The beach walls, called groynes, were made of bundled batches of hawthorn combined with baked clay, which withstood salt very well. This traditional sea defence was continued until fairly recently and you can see residual elements of it at low tide near the Mary Stanford lifeboat house at Rye Nature Reserve.

Despite the limitations of Rye's witchcraft trials, Rye had its own courts that could deal with many kinds of crimes and the records show a typical set of local crimes for the year 1618:

Killing calves too early, throwing the water from the washing of clothes at someone's door, leaving his privy and dunghill open to the annoyance of passersby, going up and down the Strand with a knotted sheet upon his head and holding a cudgel for a reason not known, making a dunghill in the churchyard, refusing to make candles for the church even though he had the fat from three butchers, leaving timber on the town's ground and shouting at the jury that they did not know what they were at, flinging filth upon graves in the churchyard, throwing water onto the heads of people walking to the fish market, encouraging men to swear in a public house, and ominously, that the Mayor of Rye did throw dirt over the wall into the house where a Huguenot lived.

In the early 1600s there was a renowned genius in Rye, a polymath skilled in Latin, Greek, Hebrew, rhetoric, logic, poetry, natural philosophy, arithmetic, geometry, cosmography, astronomy, theology, physics, dialtry (probably prophecy), navigation, calligraphy, stenography, drawing, heraldry, and history. This is the famous Samuel Jeake who built a storehouse, now known as Jeake's House in Mermaid Street, who taught his son all these things.

The poet Oliver Goldsmith wrote lines that would suit Jeake:

'And still we gazed, and still the wonder grew,

That one small head could carry all he knew'.

We have seen before that the persecution of the Huguenots lead to a stream of refugees arriving at Rye harbour. It seems that Jeake's father Henry was a baker and refugee who settled in Rye and opened a baker's shop. Henry married the daughter of the Reverend John Pearson of Peasmarsh. In 1623 Samuel Jeake was born and was found to be exceedingly clever. In 1640 his father sold the baker's shop in Rye High Street to Thomas Flinte of Ashford for £60.00 (now £12,335.00). Samuel Jeake decided to explore every aspect of science and astrology, just like Dr John Dee, and Sir Isaac Newton. He also became a diarist and his writings have been preserved and are considered very valuable.

Jeake's House - originally built as a storehouse.

In 1627, the Mayor of Rye, John Sharpe asked the government for money to save the harbour and repair walls and jetties. He explained that Rye was a key harbour for journeys to France and the town produced fish for the Royal table. He asked for £3,000.00, and that is now worth an eye-watering £673,000.

Jeake in turn had a son called Samuel born in 1652, taught at home by his father. When he left home, he worked as a wool staple merchant and moneylender. He married a girl of thirteen years, said to be a beauty but also very bright and they took over a home eventually called the Old Hospital in Mermaid Street. In 1689 Samuel Jeake the Younger built a house opposite what is now Jeake's House with astronomical symbols of the Twelve Planets that were thought to exist at the time. He in turn had a son in 1697 who gained notoriety for inventing a flying machine, a model of which was kept at Rye school. So, the whole family retained their genius from their Huguenot origins combined with the cleverness of their English spouses.

In 1637, Camber Castle was finally abandoned when King Charles I ordered its closure. When Oliver Cromwell realised that it could be used by Royalists, he partly demolished it. Nevertheless, some military assets remained there.

In the period 1636 -1638 Thomas Peacocke left in his Will a building he had constructed in the High Street. It became Thomas Peacocke School and you can read more about this in the Description of Historic Sites at the start of this Guide.

Camber Castle was now an abandoned ruin far from the sea due to huge shingle banks forming. This did not bode well for Rye Harbour. This expensive fort became permanently redundant and so the weapons, powder and provisions had to be repositioned. On 30 August 1642 an order was issued for the ammunition in the Castle of Camber, to be removed to Rye by Captain Richard Cockarem and the inhabitants of Rye.

On 24th December (Christmas Eve) 1643, the Mayor and Jurats of Rye wrote to the Committee for Sussex telling them that the castle roofing lead might be stolen 'due to the unguarded ruination of the fort'.

'We have thought good to let you know that the Castle, called Camber Castle, neere to our towne is soe greatlie ruinated and broken that any man may goe in there and purloigne and take from thence the tymber and leade; and therefore it will be verie fitt (as we conceive) that some course may be taken that the leade and such tymber as may be easilie embeazeled be taken away from thence and put in safe custodie where you shall thinke fitt to appoint'.

Then just after Christmas, on 27th December 1643 an order came from Lewes from the Committee for Sussex to the Mayor and Jurats of Rye. It was an order for six of the biggest and most serviceable pieces of ordnance in Rye to be conveyed to Shoreham, along the Sussex coast.

On 25th January 1644, the Mayor and Jurats of Rye wrote to the Committee for Sussex at Lewes. It is fascinating to read the spelling of those days even if it is a little hard to understand what people are writing.

'Concerning the removinge of the lead in Camber Castle, the wheather hath ben so unseasonable that as yet there is but litle of it brought away but there hath ben a watch day and night for securinge it ever since order from you. And we intend, with all convenience, to bringe away the rest which when it is done you shall have spedie notice. We have received a letter from Nicholas Shinner, employed by us to convey our ordnance to Shorham which you sent for, referring him to us to pay the fraight and other charges, for that the last tax imposed upon our towne is not fullie paied in of which 53l. is paid into the receivers at Battle and the residue cannot be collected by distresse, but by warrant from yourselfes to our collectors'.

In 1651 Samuel Jeake became Rye's Town Clerk but in 1656 he was forced to resign, maybe because he had become a non-conformist preacher (according to British Parliamentary History Online). Nevertheless, he remained very active in the town and in 1666/7 he drew a map of Rye showing many features including the Old Vicarage.

In 1672 there was an unusual case of an insult to King Charles II who was known to have mistresses. On 13th May, Richard

Cooper gave evidence against the wife (not named) of Richard Gravener, that she had 'hung a horn and a branch of an apple tree and some white blossom in the Strandgate having said that these were the King's colours'. These symbols, the horn, the apple branch, and blossom were symbols derived from Adam and Eve in the Garden of Eden and the goddess Astarte alluding to sexual practices of the king. So, Mrs Gravener was shamed by being made to stand in the marketplace for one hour from 11am to 12am with a piece of paper fixed to her dress above her breast stating her crime.

All this time, ships were being wrecked along the shoreline from Winchelsea and Rye to Dungeness. A strong-minded freeman of Rye named John Allen was brave enough to criticise the management of the harbour and the state of the coast where the waves were altering the shoreline in a dangerous way. It is said the harbour controllers, Trinity House, refused to accept his criticisms at a time when one thousand bodies had been collected from wrecks at Dungeness alone. All he asked for was a lighthouse. Eventually he won and a coal-fired light was set up at Dungeness.

In 1679 more witchcraft was discovered: Alicia Martin wife of Henry Martin a brazier of Rye was accused of acts against the King Charles II on 23rd December, namely:

'...that on divers days before and after, not having God before her eyes, but at the instigation of the Devil, practised and pursued certain detestable and devilish acts known in English as witchcraft and sorcery'.

By 1682, a semaphore signaling system to aid river navigation was in place and working well. It seems that Rye had an optical semaphore long before the supposed invention of it by the Frenchman Claude Chappe in 1792.

The French came along the coast firing their guns and fire ships had to be deployed to scare them off. They attacked Hastings and killed a small number of people by firing lead shot into the town from the sea. England combined with Holland to defeat them and in 1692, the Anglo-Dutch fleet attacked the French fleet anchored at Cherbourg and La Hogue thus rendering the enemy fleet fully useless for many years.

In truth, the great enemies of Rye over the centuries are shingle and silt. In a sad end to the century, the fiasco of 'Smeaton's Harbour' was still ongoing and in 1698 the Commissioners of the Navy and Elder Brethren of Trinity House said that 'Rye Harbour is effectively lost'.

CHAPTER 17

A Doomed Harbour Project

We now move to the reign of Queen Anne who was crowned in 1702 and died in 1714. During her reign England and Scotland became Great Britain. In 1705, the office of the King's Bailiff was now held by the Mayor of Rye so that he (almost certainly) or she (unheard of for years) may have two maces borne before them in civic processions.

Rye was still much of an island and there were several ferries in operation. In 1700 the building known as the Ferry Boat Inn was completed and later leased for one thousand years to Edward Doge, a carpenter, and in 1719 the George Hotel was reallocated to the current building from elsewhere.

The advent of 1722 saw James Lamb completing 'Lamb's House'. He was a rich wine merchant and politician. Historic England explains:

'King George I was entertained at Lamb House in 1726 and the Duke of Cumberland in 1757. A tablet on the house records that Henry James, Author, lived there from 1898-1916. Subsequently E F Benson, Author, lived there for some years until his death in 1940. The house suffered bomb damage mainly in the back part of the addition. Except in the northeast corner the damage to the house itself was not structural, but the single-storey building attached to the house at the south east corner and known as the Court House or Garden Room was entirely demolished.'

In 1726, King George I was in a ship that was driven ashore at Camber Sands by a storm. Rye's mayor, James Lamb gave him accommodation in Lamb House in his own bedroom while Lamb's wife in another room gave birth to a baby boy, inevitably named George and the king became the child's godfather.

Rye was willing to do almost anything to keep its access to the sea despite the failure of its harbour. The Act of Parliament of 1723 set out the idea that the Rivers Brede, Tillingham and Rother could be forced through the marshes at the back of Winchelsea to reach the sea, thus saving Rye's trade. In 1724, with a new sense of urgency work started on the 'New Harbour'. Almost immediately the situation descended into a fiasco, said to be 'marked by incompetence, indecision, financial difficulties, rivalry, and nepotism'. All the correspondence and accounts concerning this nightmare have been lost but the Minute Books remain.

To make matters worse, smuggling was rife, so much so that law-abiding citizens of Rye feared for their lives, and, as Rudyard Kipling would later write, people 'turned their faces to the wall while the gentlemen rode by'. From 1730 to 1747, the murderous Hawkhurst Gang were active in Rye, often drinking in the Mermaid Inn and the Red Lion with their feet up on the tables and their guns at the ready.

In 1742 a butcher named John Breads occupied the first Flushing Inn. This was a time when Rye was divided by attitudes to religion and ways of worship, and some people resented the upper classes of the town. Breads' home is now Number 4 Market Street, and Rye has become notorious for the story of the murder of Allen Grebell. This is a famous Rye story because it was so shocking, so it is worth setting it in context.

Rye had a mayor supported by freemen who helped to counsel and make decisions. Back in 1724 on 12th May when the harbour was causing so much concern, it was decided to form a new Harbour Commission and the town's leading lights were appointed. Here are their names: Mayor James Lamb, Thomas

Grebell, Allen Grebell, Samuel Jeake and Thomas Frewen. This was around nineteen years before a terrible mistake led to the brutal murder of the wrong man.

On 16th March 1743, James Lamb was Rye Town mayor once more. Overall he was Mayor of Rye fourteen times and was so honoured that he was one of the people who could hold the Royal Canopy over the king. He was naturally invited to dinner to celebrate his son's admission into the Customs Service. Allen Grebell was his brother-in-law. Lamb was unwell and decided he could not go to the dinner but felt that because his son was being honoured, a family member should certainly represent him. Because it was March, it was still cold and so Lamb gave Grebell his mayoral cloak. It is said that John Breads had been fined by Lamb, in his role as magistrate, for giving short weights of meat and this generated a hatred but there was, because of religious differences, a certain 'us-and-them' resentment between a common tradesman and a mayor.

So, when Breads found out that Lamb was to go to his son's celebratory dinner, he lay in wait for him in St Mary's Churchyard with a large butcher's knife. As Grebell, dressed like Lamb would have been, crossed Rye churchyard on his return home, so Breads leapt out and stabbed him, then ran. Grebell, somewhat inebriated yet mortally wounded, staggered to his home. It is thought he did not realise he had been stabbed and fell asleep in his chair and bled out. The following morning he was discovered dead by his man-servant who was initially suspected of the crime.

Yet it was soon obvious to all who had done this terrible thing. Legend has it that Breads was heard claiming 'Butchers should kill Lambs' and in the urgency of arrest Breads blurted out that he had meant to kill Mayor Lamb. Breads was taken to the prison section of the Ypres Tower. Lamb was related through marriage to victim Grebell so he should have taken no part in the investigation, but in his fury Lamb seems to have broken the law or at least its strong guidance that he should not be judge of a case where a relative had been murdered. But Lamb knew he was the intended victim and so it seems he manipulated the law to become, first – the coroner for Grebell's body, and then chief prosecutor of Breads, and then his case judge. Some historians feel that he may well have given evidence as well, and these acts would have been a fully illegal breach of Common Law today, making any current trial a legal impossibility.

Yes, Breads was guilty, but you can see the fury that must have gripped Lamb, because he then exceeded his powers when he sentenced Breads to death by hanging with the additional sentence that his body was to be gibbeted – hung in a cage at Gibbet's Marsh near the Tillingham tide gate windmill that you can see from Rye Heritage Centre today. Gibbetting usually needed a royal order.

Breads' skull still is trapped inside the gibbet cage which is still to this day kept in Rye Town Hall. His body was left to rot in public for decades, some of his bones being taken and ground up for cures for rheumatism. There is another side to the murder and the actions of Lamb. In a June 1743 edition of the Kentish Post, some details of the trial emerged in print where it was claimed that Breads had said that he had no idea how or why he had tried to kill Lamb, and ended up killing Grebell, because he was insane. The newspaper reported the words, 'If I have done this act, I knew nothing of it because I was in a state of distraction'. Legal minds who have looked at the case have said it was possible that Breads might have been sent to a mental institution instead of being hanged for committing a crime while the balance of his mind was disturbed. However, looking at the totality of the story it seems that the power of a mayor of Rye in the 18th century was almost infinite. John Breads was the last man to be hanged in Rye, in 1743.

The River Tillingham has a strong flow, enough to flood Rye's Strand Quay when the tide is in and it has rained hard up country. Yet right next to the river there has been a windmill for many years, styled as a 'smock mill' from the shape of its wide lower outline. In 1758, Thomas Chatterton took ownership of this landmark Rye Windmill at Gibbet's Marsh. In those days there were no tide gates that could be shut to prevent flooding and more to the point there was easy access to the Rother river and the sea. Rye's characteristic pitch-painted shallow draft barges plied the river. The very last one, a huge vessel called Primrose, is currently being restored at the Shipwreck Museum in Hastings.

In 1762, despite all the infighting and corruption, the 'New Harbour' was being cleared and the sea was finally to be let into part of the harbour to the point where it met the River Brede. But something was wrong! So, in 1763, John Smeaton FRS, was brought in as consultant. Smeaton said that ideally the cut should be to the north of the town of Winchelsea, but the commissioners ignored this and ordered the cut to be made to the south. Poor Smeaton goes down in history as the designer of a total fiasco, but it was not his fault at all.

Nevertheless, on 25th June 1787 the Admiralty Commissioners ordered the closure of 'Old' Rye Harbour from 14th July. 'Smeaton's' New Harbour was now to be used by order of the government. Inevitably, in the very next autumn and approaching winter, the raging sea and storms brought silt and shingle into 'Smeaton's' harbour mouth. The sea broke onto the land and the water, almost like a tsunami, rushed up the New Harbour entrance to Scott's Float, thus ruining the formal opening of the harbour. This pathetic and expensive enterprise lasted around three months. One large ship of 200 tons, the cutter *Salisbury,* managed to pass through the channel called on maps 'New Harbour Canal'. Then silt returned.

A Rye vessel seen in the harbour with the town of Rye in the distance

Consequently, the land drainage system failed and there was mass flooding to the point where the local population start to panic that their livelihoods would be ruined, and lives would be lost. So, on the 6th of November 1787, reality finally hit the people of Rye and they now saw clearly how they had been led not by lions but by asses. The 'New Harbour' was abandoned, and all the workmen were sacked. But never say never, the government moved in to rectify things, simply because Rye was an important port so near to France. After two years hard work, in April 1789, the people of Rye said thanks to the commissioners for giving them their old harbour back!

Back in 1778, the Rye to London Mail Coach began to use the George Hotel as its venue for mail pick-up and delivery.

Now the old harbour was being used once more and ships and boats must pay taxes for import and exports, hence the popularity of smuggling to avoid payment. In 1790 it is thought that the Custom House, known as Grene Hall, was planned, and then completed by 1810. It may have been a refurbished building dating back to c.1480, or a newbuild on that site.

During the 17th Century, Rye continued its traditional trade of pottery production. Local craftsmen and those fleeing from France came to Rye to make a unique type of pottery called 'hopware', where hop leaves and the actual hops themselves were incorporated into the clay.

High import taxes ensured that smuggling continued apace, and the 'owling' trade developed. The Owlers were men who hooted signals to their colleagues to warn of the Revenue men who were chasing them. It was a capital offence to cover your face to prevent law and order from identifying you. However, the smugglers of Rye and Romney, full of bravado, wore what was called 'bee-skeps' and other types of eye-slitted balaclavas or masks to prevent identification. There was so much money to be made from the illegal export of wool and a ready market in France was so near. Now that wool was so popular as contraband, along came tea and so now there was something else to smuggle.

*Rye Harbour and Camber Sands - see here from the end of the
Harbour Arm*

Rye harbour was now very busy, and it was important to avoid
navigation accidents. Tides and weather had to be considered.
But how to alert sailors and fisherfolk to problems? It was not
sensible to rely on fire beacons to signal from hilltop to hilltop,
but there were lighthouses.

Then in 1792, 100 years after Rye's first signaling system shown
on maps of 1692, a bright spark in France called Claude Chappe
invented a more sophisticated ship semaphore – the terrestrial
semaphore telegraph. This chap was a clergyman. His invention
used pivoted arms, a bit like the railway signals we see today.
Rye harbour soon had new towers, arms, and cables to be
able to send codes out to sea. The design of telescopes had
greatly improved and ships at sea could see the Rye harbour
semaphore system which told them of the tides and hazards in
a code that all the boat owners adopted. If there was fog or other
adverse weather, then ship's crews had to fend for themselves
as nothing could be done until the invention of radio.

In Rye, the Ypres Tower gun garden weaponry was re-armed and supplied to ensure an effective defence against the French. On 15th August 1769, a child was born in Corsica to descendants of a noble Italian family. He became Emperor Napoleon, and his actions changed the landscape around Rye forever.

River Rother - Simmons Quay

CHAPTER 18

The Coming of the Railway

In 1801, John Vidler bought the building known now as Friars of the Sack. The link to the building is obscure and no-one is sure that the Friars of the Penance of Jesus Christ, as they were formally known, could ever have lived there. They were only in England from 1247 to 1274 and only in Rye from 1263. However, the Vidler family is well known in Rye, and it was a Vidler who became the most prominent historian of Rye.

Napoleon became a great threat to England, and he planned to invade. At the same time there was much cross-channel smuggling traffic, and it would certainly have made sense for Napoleon's spies to have infiltrated the smuggling gangs.

Successive prime ministers tried to convince parliament that smuggling was caused by high import taxes and that if these were reduced or removed, then the illegal and murderous trade would cease. William Pitt the Younger worked hard during the late 18th and early 19th centuries to change the taxation system. He had discovered that in 1784 alone thirteen million pounds weight of tea came into the country but only 5.5 million pounds weight were imported legally. By the time Pitt decided to act, twenty per cent of all imports came into the nation illegally and it was smugglers who brought in half of all the tea in England. Tea was so expensive and precious that leading householders would keep the key to the tea caddy on a chain around their necks. Pitt the Younger dropped the tax on tea from 119% to 25%. However, when Napoleon was defeated and captured, the Navy had the time and ships to crack down on the smugglers and the coastguard helped during the period from 1815 through to 1840 when the reduction in taxation took most of the profit out of smuggling.

While the smuggling was rife so was the fear of invasion. During the period 1803 to 1805 Napoleon assembled a truly massive invasion force of 350,000 well-trained men with superb leadership and most significantly, the inclusion of the magnificent Imperial Guard. This was the *Grande Armée*, of seven corps, cavalry, and artillery – a sight to fear and behold. They could almost be seen from Dover on a clear day as they were assembled at Boulogne. A huge fleet of 1,300 shallow draft barges were built to carry the troops. It was like the Norman invasion all over again. Senior French officers asked Napoleon for permission to mount 1,000-men raids on coastal settlements and harbours from Hastings to Folkestone.

While Admiral Nelson and the Duke of Wellington were active in defence, it was decided to build a canal – the Royal Military Canal, right across Romney Marsh and the Dungeness promontory. Romney Marsh was flat grassland and Dungeness with its vast shingle terrain, the largest in Europe, was seen as the best and flattest access to the English countryside and its terrified population.

In late 1804, the canal was suggested and then designed by Lieutenant-Colonel John Brown of the Royal Staff Corps of Field Engineers. It was a preferable alternative to deliberately flooding all the Romney Marsh farmland to stop the enemy. The Duke of York and William Pitt the Younger thought the idea brilliant and Pitt came to Romney Marsh to convince the landowners. John Rennie was appointed to oversee the project and the first cut was at Seabrook, near Hythe.

But despite the imminent risk of invasion, only six miles of canal had been built by May 1805. Pitt sacked Rennie and the Army took over, with navvies doing the digging and soldiers making the ramparts. A road was made alongside the canal and gun batteries were installed. A set of moveable wooden bridges helped the workmen to move from bank to bank as progress was made. The canal was finished in April 1809 at a total cost of £234,000. Now this sum today would be £17 million. This was not the only expense because a series of Martello Towers were also built to defend the coast, some of which can still be seen. A system of canal tolls was set up to help pay back the investment.

Yet Nelson had defeated the French fleet at Cape Trafalgar on 21st October 1805, wrecking French sea power and making it very unlikely, in fact almost impossible, that they would invade after all. Nevertheless, it took ten more years of hard fighting until the Battle of Waterloo on 18th June 1815 to finish off this French dictator for good.

Once Napoleon was safely imprisoned on the South Atlantic Island of St Helena, then the people of Rye could return to a state of happiness and personal enjoyment – and a sign of this was that in 1818 a ballroom was added to the George Hotel.

In 1826, Rye Corporation decided to supply a new water pump at Pump Street near Church Square, and the 'Rat's Tail' pump spout can be seen there today. In 1830, with the threat of invasion long past, it was decided not to continue maintenance of the weaponry and ammunition at the Ypres Tower and some of the eighteen guns were removed.

There were other significant changes in Rye. In 1830, Rye had its Gasworks. In 1837 the Ypres Tower prison was given a woman's prison section – and in 1850, the railway finally arrived with a train full of eager passengers turning up even before the station building had been completed.

In 1850, the Irishman William H Balls arrived to implement strict law and order. He was the man who set up the police patrol system in Rye and he worked here for 30 years.

In 1865, when the Salvation Army was formed, the Augustinian chapel became their 'barracks' until they moved into the Citadel on Rope Walk.

Ypres Tower prison was closed in 1891 and in 1898 Rye needed much more water, so a bore hole was drilled at Cadborough Cliff in 1898.

Rye Signal Box - a Grade II Listed Building refurbished in 2019 by Network Rail.

CHAPTER 19

Twentieth Century – Wars and Floods

The First World War began in 1914 and lasted until 1918. During that time millions died fighting over tiny pieces of poppy-strewn land in Flanders and elsewhere.

John Collard's book, *A Maritime History of Rye (1985)* details the trials and tribulations of our town. Rye soon found that war produced refugees when a series of Belgian fishing boats brought families from Ostend to Folkestone and then along the coast. This war reduced revenue to the harbour as trade was lessened, but the Rye barges were busy moving war goods.

In 1916 there was a great explosion in the Bay when the steam trawler 'Margaret Colebrook' hit a mine. A German submarine captured a Rye vessel, the 'Gazelle' near the Sovereign lightship. The Germans put the crew off in a small boat and blew the Rye boat up. Many people from Rye died on European shores and the harbour revenue dropped to the point where it was once again on the point of closing for good, but with help from the Treasury and a small local tax, it was saved.

A few years after the First World War ended, a series of storms created a huge shingle bank across the harbour mouth, causing vessels attempting to dock to b e driven aground and often wrecked, including a 200-ton coaster.

Then there came a much greater disaster when on 15th November 1928, the Lithuanian vessel *SS Alice of Riga* signalled to the radio station on the North Foreland that she was in trouble in heavy seas. North Foreland quite sensibly tried to call out the Dungeness lifeboat but was unable to get through so alerted the Mary Stanford lifeboat crew at Rye Harbour. In appalling weather conditions the crew and launchers ran the mile and a half from the village to the lifeboat house on the shore-line and, brave as hell, into the surf they went, seventeen men at the oars and helm with the sail up, desperately searching for the *Alice*.

Gradually the wind rose to a massive gale with the sea building mountains of water and yet the Mary Stanford kept on searching. Back on shore they had received a message saying that the Alice had been sighted and that rescue was at hand from another steamer. Three recall rockets were fired. However, there was no way that the crew of the Mary Stanford could receive this message as the gale was blinding to any kind of visibility, so all the shore hands could do was wait – and then the horrific sight of the upturned Mary Stanford came in view.

Every single crew member was lost, one body never being recovered – all local men with families so the grief was intense. A fund was created to help the families. This reached £30,000 which today is equivalent to £1.5 million pounds. The Mary Stanford lifeboat house stands on the far shore of the Rye Harbour Nature Reserve today, but the sea is eating towards its foundations and unless something is done, it too will go into the sea.

Mary Stanford Lifeboat House

Despite the war, with the coming of the railway, Rye's commerce potential grew. It was clear that modern times were here because in 1910, Rye's first cinema opened, known as 'The Flea Pit'. It was closed in 1932 and replaced by the Regent Cinema. In the period 1926/27, Spanish style came to Rye when the John Mendham, who had lived in Argentina, was asked to design St Anthony Padua (Roman Catholic) church in Watchbell Street in the Spanish Colonial style.

Author Radclyffe Hall gave a cross to that church. She was the lover first of Mabel Batten and then Mabel's cousin Una, Lady Troubridge. Nowadays we celebrate the fact that at last people can express themselves without it being a criminal offence, but back in those days, such untoward' sexual activities were looked at with suspicion, horror, or disgust by some, and as exciting bravado by others, trapped in their strait-laced lives.

Rye's reputation for ceramics was expanded to become a centre for art and literature. With the railway now providing easier access to Rye compared with the twisting country roads, people began to see Rye as a very pleasant prospect nestling between beautiful countryside and the sea and marshes where peace and tranquillity could aid ideas in art and literature.

The lives and works of the writers, artists and actors who made their homes in Rye would fill a book, but here is a sample. We have already mentioned Henry James (1843-1916) who came to Rye in the 1890s. Radclyffe Hall (1880-1943) authored a brave novel about lesbianism called 'The Well of Loneliness'. After a trial, the book was ordered to be burned, but the text survived to be republished.

Conrad Aiken (1889-1973) was an American poet, who authored novels and acted as a literary critic. He moved to Rye in 1921. Writer Monica Edwards (Monica le Doux Newton) (1912-1998) lived at Rye Harbour. A.C. Benson (1862-1925) was also an author and poet, and his brother E.F. Benson (1867-1940) wrote novels and biographies and gave money to help Rye develop. John Christopher (1922-2012) came to live in Rye in the 1960s – he was a science fiction writer.

Malcolm Saville (1901-1982) wrote children's books including the '*Lone Pine*' series, and John Ryan (1921-2009) also wrote children's books, notably *Captain Pugwash*, but additionally was an artist and illustrator.

As far as art is concerned, Anthony Van Dyk (1599-1641) from Holland worked in Rye in the 17th century drawing Rye in detail. J.M.W. Turner (1775-1851) painted for the Victorians, producing some romantic views of the landscapes of Rye and Winchelsea. Later, Edward Burra (1905-1976) was born in Rye and went on to become a unique artist. Rye Art Gallery is home to several significant works.

John Banting (1902-1972) was a painter and writer who lived in Rye in the 1950s at No 10, High Street. The architect, Frederick Edward Bradshaw MacManus OBE (1903- 1985) retired to live in Rye. Geoffrey Bagley (1901-1992) was a Canadian war artist who continued his work in Rye to preserve its great heritage.

Rother Bridge

World War II

The rescue of the British Expeditionary Force from Dunkirk on 4th June 1940 has been hailed as a triumph snatched from the teeth of disaster. A truly amazing 309,000 troops were rescued from Dunkirk beaches and a further 192,000 men, women and children were saved from beaches along the coasts of France. Rye boats helped, going first to Ramsgate where the English Channel was at its narrowest point for a sail to Dunkirk. One Rye registered trawler, the *Dorothy Margaret*, took off 100 men in one journey alone.

By June 1940 it was clear that the Nazis were relentless, efficient, and led by a maniac, so invasion was expected across a wide area from Ramsgate to Dorset with overwhelming force. The British coastal population would be softened up by bombing. Then the Nazis began to wonder if the design of the invasion front was too wide and that the force applied would be diluted. Hitler decided to scrap the plan and concentrate on a section of the Kent and Sussex coast alone in Operation Sealion. Hitler targeted Rye Bay as being ideal and that fact was discovered, leaving the Royal Sussex Regiment to cover a huge area including Dungeness. Some areas were mined, some plans were made to set the sea on fire with oil. Howitzers were sited and manned as everyone waited for the hammer blow to come. But that blow could only come after the bombers and fighters of the German Air Force had softened up the English coast – and that never happened because the Royal Air Force, during what is now called the Battle of Britain, reduced the Nazi air capability sufficiently to give Hitler second thoughts.

This total failure of Operation Sealion was psychologically significant, and it helped senior politicians and planning officers to think how the British and their allies could mount an invasion of France and Germany. Orders for total secrecy were given and all sorts of false defences were created. Camber Sands was used as an invasion practice ground. Field Marshal Montgomery came to Rye to inspect troops and even Prime Minister Winston Churchill passed close by. On 6th June

1944, Operation Overlord began, despite the flying bombs and rockets. The tide was turning in our favour and eventually we won, and peace returned.

However, top secret work done in the USA at Alamogordo, and the subsequent bombing of Hiroshima and Nagasaki projected Rye into the nuclear age and now on the horizon east of Camber Sands looms the grey hulk of Dungeness Nuclear Power Station.

Rye Fish for sale

CHAPTER 20

Present Day

Now Rye celebrates its past with displays at Rye Museum and Rye Heritage Centre. You can learn much of Rye's rich history by visiting Rye Heritage Centre and seeing the amazing Story of Rye sound and light show, featuring the famous large scale Rye Town Model telling of many events of the past as described in this Town Guide. You can also get a flavour of Rye smugglers' nefarious pursuits in the newly opened Smuggler's Attic multimedia experience.

Rye Museum continues the story through the use of numerous displays and artefacts in its two sites at the Ypres Tower and East Street.

The town is busy with fishing, sailing, art, commerce, festivals and tourism.

The wonderful Rye Harbour Nature Reserve is a site of special scientific interest (SSSI) managed by Sussex Wildlife Trust, with a superbly-designed Discovery Centre, cafeteria and shop. There is also a nearby free car park (donations encouraged) run by Icklesham Parish Council. There are paths to be explored and bird hides to be used for observation of a remarkable variety of avian species. The shingle area is fenced to keep out foxes and badgers so that ground nesting birds can lay their eggs safely. Thanks to a wonderful piece of thoughtful engineering, the road to the Discovery Centre has a tunnel underneath it that allows the rising tide to spread into a vast salt marsh. You can watch the ebb and flow of the tide from the Discovery Centre's huge glass windows and see the thousands of birds wheeling and swooping in their many murmurations across the marshes.

Iconic Red-roofed hut on the Nature Reserve

Nature Reserve Panorama

Rye is such a wonderful and fascinating place with so much to enjoy that many residents want it kept a secret. To see the whole of the town, why not spend a small fee and climb up the tower of the St Mary's Church via the bell loft, where you will see a breathtaking vast panorama of sea, land, and sky.

CHAPTER 21

Walks

Town and Local Walks

At Rye Heritage Centre you will find booklets with details of local walks and cycle rides, the Town Trail map detailing 21 places of historical interest within the town and find out about guided walks and when they are available.

Walk to Camber Sands

You can leave the town by the bridge over the Rother and follow the signs to Camber Sands where you will see one of the largest dunes systems in Britain and much wildlife.

Camber Sands

Winchelsea

Also nearby is Winchelsea, where the ancient wine cellars can be visited and you can also go into the church of St Thomas Becket and see the stained-glass windows dedicated to the loss of the Mary Stanford lifeboat, and the tomb of Gervase Alard, the first Admiral of the Cinque Ports. The 1066 Country Walk starts at the edge of Gibbet Marsh and there are numerous footpaths to explore including to the ruins of Camber Castle. Walking guide books and maps are available to buy at Rye Heritage Centre where you may also be able to book onto a guided walk of the town (see above).

Rye Harbour Wildlife Reserve Walks

Rye Harbour Nature Reserve is home to over 4,355 species of animals and plants, including rare and endangered ones and some remarkable sights can be experienced here.

Rye Harbour Nature Reserve's Discovery Centre and Cafe

Circular Walks: The reserve offers several circular walks with varying lengths:

Short Circular Route (3.3 km or 2 miles): This wheelchair and pushchair-friendly route passes three birdwatching hides and provides frequent benches for resting.

Cormorants near a bird hide

Medium Circular Route (6.9 km or 4.3 miles): Includes a visit to the Mary Stanford Lifeboat House and a return along the shingle track through Rye Harbour farm.

Long Circular Route (9.7 km or 6.0 miles): Takes you to Camber Castle, a nearby birdwatching hide, and a viewpoint.

Winchelsea Beach Car Park Route (4.8 km or 3.0 miles)

Rye Heritage Centre thanks you for reading

Chapter 22

Weblinks

www.ryeheritage.co.uk

www.ryemuseum.co.uk

www.ryesussex.org

www.visit1066country.com

www.easyfundraising.org.uk/causes/ryeheritagecentre

https://www.giveasyoulive.com/charity/rye-heritage-centre

https://lossenham.org.uk/

The St Mary's Rye Town Clock Controversy:

https://ahs.contentfiles.net/media/documents/Salisbury_Well
s_and_Rye__great_clocks_revisited_IIqtQXb.pdf

CHAPTER 23

Acknowledgements

For their help in producing this guide we would like

to acknowledge the following:

Rye Heritage Centre volunteers and trustees

Paul Goring

Jenny Hadfield

Stephen Masters

Domain Support

The Rotary Club of Rye and Winchelsea

All photographs by David EP Dennis except for:

Pages 14, 42 and 126 – The Pilcher Collection by kind permission
of Dymchurch Heritage Association.

Smugglers image in Rye Heritage Centre advertisement –
Copyright by Corin Spinks.

Milton Keynes UK
Ingram Content Group UK Ltd.
UKHW030953120824
446802UK00009B/136